UNSEEN AND BEYOND

HOW TO BECOME YOUR DREAM SELF

SIMRAN MOHANTY

To all those who believe in their dreams.

To my parents for their undeterred support.

And, to my baby niece, Tishya.

Contents

Contents

Preface

Pause.

Let's pause for a moment and talk about the word *becoming*. It's one of those simple words that holds worlds of meaning. To become something is not just about wanting it or working toward it. It's about stepping into the version of yourself who already is that.

But how do we *"become"* something that feels so far away? Here's where the unseen and beyond comes in. You see, we tend to live in a very visible, tangible world—one where we focus on what we can see, touch, and prove. Yet the true magic of life lies in the unseen: energy, vibrations, intentions, and the infinite potential of the Universe. These are the forces quietly shaping everything around us, whether we notice them or not.

When I first started writing this book, I had to learn this lesson myself. I'd sit staring at a blank page, doubting whether I was "really" a writer. One day, it hit me: writers write. Full stop. So, I stopped questioning and just started doing. I'd visualize my name on the cover of a book and feel the pride and joy as if it's already happened. I trusted that the right words, the right opportunities, and the right readers would show up at the perfect time. And guess what? They did. That shift—choosing to embody the identity before the world gave me proof—was a game-changer.

This is where manifestation often surprises people—it isn't about waiting for your external world to change before you feel different. It's about first feeling and embodying the change internally, and then watching your reality shift to match. And that's why becoming is so powerful. It's not about faking it until you make it; it's about aligning your entire being with the energy of your desire.

When you do this, you're not just wishing or hoping—you're actively participating in the creation of your reality. The unseen isn't just a mystical concept; it's rooted in the very fabric of the Universe.

Think about gravity.

You can't see it, but you trust it implicitly. You don't question whether the Earth will hold you when you step out of bed in the morning—it just does. The same goes for the Law of Attraction and the energy you emit. Just because you can't see these forces doesn't mean they aren't constantly at work.

And, science backs this up. Quantum physics tells us that everything in the Universe is made up of energy. Even the solid objects around you—your phone, your chair, your morning coffee—are, at their core, vibrating particles. Your thoughts and emotions vibrate, too. They send out signals, like ripples in a pond, that interact with the energy of everything else.

The Universe isn't just passively observing your vibrations—it's responding to them. It's aligning people, opportunities, and circumstances to match the frequency you're broadcasting.

This is the unseen at work. And when you consciously tune your energy to align with what you want, you begin to move beyond the limits of what you thought was possible.

Take Wi-Fi, for example. You can't see the signals flying around, but they're there, connecting you to the world. Manifestation operates on the same principle. The energy you put out—the thoughts, feelings, and intentions you carry—is constantly "broadcasting" and shaping your reality.

When I wanted to live with more abundance, I stopped treating money like a problem and started treating it like a partner. I'd thank my bills for the services they provided and celebrate every paycheck, no matter the size. The energy I sent out was one of gratitude and trust—and the Universe matched it with more opportunities than I ever imagined.

Here's another example: imagine you want to attract love. Instead of waiting for *"the one"* to sweep you off your feet, you become the kind of person who embodies love. You take yourself on dates. You treat yourself with kindness and respect. You radiate the energy of someone who knows they're deeply lovable. And in doing so, you naturally draw love toward you—because like attracts like.

What makes becoming so transformative is that it allows you to live beyond the limits of what you can see right now. It asks you to trust in something greater than yourself—the energy of the Universe, the magic of the unseen.

And trust me, this is where the real magic lies. When you start living as though your desires are already yours, you create a powerful ripple effect that touches everything and everyone around you.

This book, Unseen and Beyond is exactly about that—learning to see beyond the surface of your current reality and tapping into the invisible forces that are always working in your favor. It's about stepping into your highest potential and realizing that the Universe isn't out there somewhere—it's within you.

As you read this book, I invite you to approach it with curiosity and openness. You don't have to have all the answers right now. You don't even have to fully believe in the unseen. All I ask is that you allow yourself to explore the possibility that there's more to life than what meets the eye.

In the chapters that follow, we'll dive deeper into how to become your manifestation and live in alignment with your desires.

You'll learn practical tools, exercises, and mindsets to help you tap into the unseen and beyond. But most importantly, you'll learn how to trust yourself and the incredible power you hold.

So, this book is divided into 6 parts, each designed to guide you deeper into the art of becoming:

Part 1: BUILD

Manifestation begins with you. Who you are determines what you attract. This section will help you redefine your self-concept, teaching you to become the version of yourself capable of receiving your desires. You'll learn the importance of self-love and how to cultivate it through affirmations, mirror work, and daily rituals.

Part 2: BREATHE

Once you've built a strong foundation, it's time to connect with the Universe. We'll explore practices like meditation, breathwork, and chakra alignment. These tools help you align your energy with your desires, turning you into a powerful magnet for manifestation.

Part 3: BALANCE

Manifestation isn't just about wishing; it's about doing. This section focuses on inspired action—action that feels aligned and effortless. You'll also learn about the power of daily habits to keep your energy high and intentions clear.

Part 4: BRIDGE

Emotions are energy in motion, acting as a compass to guide your manifestation journey. In this part, you'll learn how to tune into your emotions, understand their messages, and use them to stay aligned with your desires.

Part 5: BREAK FREE

Even with the best intentions, limiting beliefs and emotional blocks can hold you back. This section introduces tools like EFT (Emotional Freedom Technique) and the CTFAR model to break through these barriers and clear the path for your desires.

Part 6: BECOME

The final step is to become your desire. You'll learn how to embody the person who already has what they want, raising your vibration to match your goals. This is the ultimate key to unlocking your manifestation potential.

So, let's begin.

Let's step into the unseen together and start becoming the people we were always meant to be.

How To Use This Book

Before we dive into the exciting steps that can bring your desires to life, let's take a moment to get acquainted with how this book works. Think of this chapter as your friendly roadmap, ensuring you have all the tools you need to make the most of this journey.

This book is about *you*. Your dreams, your goals, and your potential. It's divided into 6 transformative steps that stand in the way between you and your manifestation. Whether you're here to manifest the job you've always wanted, deepen a relationship, or attract abundance into your life, this process is designed to guide you step by step with clarity and intention.

To fully benefit from this book, I encourage you to keep a dedicated journal or notebook close by. You'll find a small "DIY Exercise" at the end of every chapter. These exercises are designed to help you absorb what you've learned and immediately apply it to your life. Writing things down is powerful—it transforms thoughts into tangible actions.

Come to this book with an open heart and a willingness to embrace trust. Even if manifestation feels unfamiliar or daunting right now, don't worry. With trust, intention, and effort, change will unfold naturally.

Take a moment now to think about what you'd like to manifest. Don't overthink it—listen to your heart. Is it a fulfilling job? A partner who truly understands you? A sense of peace and contentment? Close your eyes and picture it clearly. And, by the time you finish this book, you'll have completed a personal manifestation project.

This book will help you take that vision from abstract to achievable. Over the course of 18 chapters, we'll build toward that goal. Each chapter builds on the one before it, creating a step-by-step process you can follow seamlessly. Plus, you will find a P.S. (Please See) bonus section full of tips, tricks, and reminders to apply what you've learned to your daily life.

It's important to commit to these exercises and practices sincerely. You'll see the best results when you actively engage with each step.

This is your opportunity to take a leap toward the life you've always dreamed of. It's not about perfection; it's about progress. You've already taken the first step by picking up this book. The next steps will unfold one by one, as you open your mind and heart to possibility.

So, are you ready?

Let's get started.
Turn the page, and let your journey begin!

• xv •

SPEAKING THE LANGUAGE OF THE UNIVERSE
How to Manifest Your Dream Life

BUILD

I

Mechanics of Manifestation

Alright, before we dive into the first chapter, let's take a moment to get comfortable. Imagine we're sitting together, and this chapter is a conversation over your favorite drink. Coffee? Tea? Bubble tea with extra tapioca? Whatever works! Because understanding yourself isn't about dull definitions or snooze-worthy psychology. It's about real talk and the journey through self-discoverability that makes you, well, *you*! Ready to settle in? Great —let's begin.

The human mind is a labyrinth of possibilities and a compass for dreams. It's interesting how the subconscious mind, which makes up 95% of our brain activity, isn't just a passive observer—it's the architect of your reality. It's a realm where your beliefs, emotions, and memories merge into an invisible force that shapes every decision you make, every action you take, and every outcome you experience. While the conscious mind may act as the captain steering the ship, the subconscious is the vast ocean beneath, influencing the journey in ways you don't even realize.

Unlike the conscious mind, which deals with logic, reasoning, and willpower, the subconscious is a domain of automatic responses, emotions, and deeply ingrained habits. It doesn't analyze or question—it simply accepts and executes. If your subconscious is filled with empowering beliefs, it becomes a powerful ally. But if it's cluttered with doubt, fear, and negativity, it can't work in your favor.

One of the most intriguing aspects of the subconscious mind is its inability to differentiate between reality and imagination. To your subconscious, the things you repeatedly visualize, affirm, or feel emotionally are just as real as your lived experiences. This is why recurring thoughts, whether positive or negative, have such a profound impact. If you constantly tell yourself, *"I'm not good enough,"* your subconscious will internalize that belief and manifest behaviors that align with it. On the flip side, affirming, *"I am capable and deserving,"* plants a seed of confidence that blossoms over time.

From the moment you're born, your subconscious absorbs information like a sponge—family values, societal norms, cultural beliefs, and personal experiences. By the time you're 7 years old, much of your subconscious programming is already in place, acting as a filter through which you interpret the world. This programming, however, isn't set in stone. Through conscious effort, visualization, and repetition, you can rewrite these deeply embedded patterns to align with your goals and aspirations. And that is the sole purpose of this book.

WISHFUL THINKING

That's where manifestation steps in—often dismissed as mere wishful thinking, yet deeply rooted in aligning your thoughts, emotions, and actions with your goals to shape your reality. It's less about magic and more like a masterful puzzle where psychology, neuroscience, and physics intersect perfectly. The science of manifestation begins with the understanding that energy is the foundation of the Universe. Everything—whether physical objects, emotions, or thoughts—vibrates at a specific frequency. Positive emotions like joy, gratitude, and love vibrate at higher frequencies, while fear, anger, and doubt operate at lower ones. When you intentionally focus on a goal and generate high-vibrational emotions around it, you align your energy with the outcome you desire.

This alignment isn't just a metaphysical concept; it's supported by psychology. The brain's neuroplasticity—its ability to form new neural connections—plays a critical role in manifestation. When you repeatedly focus on a goal, visualize it, and emotionally connect with it, you strengthen the neural pathways associated with that desire. Over time, this makes the goal feel attainable and real, motivating you to take actions that bring it closer to fruition.

Moreover, manifestation leverages the principle of synchronicity, the meaningful coincidences that occur when your inner world aligns with the outer world. Have you ever noticed how opportunities seem to appear just when you've decided to pursue a specific goal? This isn't luck—it's the result of your focused intention amplifying your awareness of relevant opportunities. We will tap more into this in the later chapters of the book.

When quintessential elements like belief, emotional alignment, and inspired action work together, you create a powerful momentum that attracts the right circumstances, people, and resources into your life. However, above everything it requires a stringent beleif in yourself, that *you can!*

THE MAGNETIC PRINCIPLE OF LIFE

Your thoughts and emotions act as a magnet, pulling similar energies toward you.

And that is exactly what the Law of Attraction prescribes; like attracts like. The energy you project into the world is the energy you receive in return. At first glance, the Law of Attraction may seem overly simplistic—just think positively, and good things will happen.

But the reality is deeper.

It's not just about the words you say or the fleeting thoughts you have; it's about the dominant energy you carry. If you think, *"I want abundance,"* but deep down you feel scarcity and doubt, your vibrational signal is mixed. The Universe responds to your vibration, not your words.

The Law of Attraction teaches us to focus on what we want, not on what we fear. Worrying about failure, for instance, shifts your focus and energy toward failure, making it more likely to occur. By contrast, focusing on success, joy, and gratitude attracts circumstances that reflect those feelings. Manifestation is a co-creative process. While you focus on your goals and raise your vibration, you must also take practical steps toward achieving them. This synergy between belief and action is what transforms a piece of imagination to complete fruition.

THE ENGINE OF IMAGINATION

Imagination is one of the most profound and mysterious abilities of the human mind. It's not just daydreaming or an escape from reality—it's the blueprint for everything we create, achieve, and become. Every single thing that exists in the world today, from towering skyscrapers to the smartphone in your hand, was once just an idea, a fleeting thought that someone dared to imagine. This is the power of imagination—it allows us to construct and experience the reality we desire in our minds before bringing it into existence. When you imagine something, you're not just picturing it; you're mentally rehearsing its creation. You're imprinting the idea into your brain, laying the groundwork for it to become tangible.

Think about it: before a painter creates a masterpiece, they see it vividly in their mind's eye. Before an architect designs a building, they imagine its structure, its purpose, and how it will feel to stand inside it. Before scientists discover a breakthrough, they envision a world where their theory holds true. The power of imagination is not just about conjuring up fantasies—it's about mentally constructing the life you want to live and the person you want to become, thereby bridging between the invisible world of possibilities and the visible world of form.

BRINGING VISION TO LIFE

On that note, it's important to distinguish between active imagination and passive daydreaming. While daydreaming is a pleasurable escape, active imagination is a deliberate act of creation. It's purposeful and intentional, fueled by a desire to bring your vision to life.

When you use your imagination actively, you're not just drifting into fantasies—you're constructing the architecture of your future. You're deciding what you want, why you want it, and how it will feel when you achieve it. This process isn't just about dreaming big; it's about dreaming with clarity and focus.

For example, let's say you want to grow your business. Instead of vaguely imagining "success," you get specific. Imagine reaching a certain revenue milestone, building a team of talented individuals, and creating a product or service that makes a meaningful impact. You picture yourself waking up each day feeling fulfilled and excited about the work you do.

This kind of specific, vivid imagination isn't just inspiring—it's actionable. It gives your mind a clear target to aim for and helps you align your energy, actions, and intentions with that target.

‰

DIY EXERCISE

This is the first DIY Exercise for you. I call it, "Mirror work", a transformative practice that involves looking at yourself in the mirror and speaking affirmations of love, worthiness, and empowerment. It's not just about the words you say—it's about the connection you establish with yourself.

To begin, find a quiet space and stand in front of a mirror. Look into your own eyes. At first, it might feel uncomfortable, but that's okay. This discomfort is often a sign of the limiting beliefs you're about to dissolve.

Start with a simple script aligning with affirmations like:

"I am a happy individual. I am beautiful. I love myself. I am worthy and deserving of all the love, abundance, and happiness that the Universe has to offer.

I matter. I am enough. I am proud of everything I have achieved in my life. I am divinely guided, protected, and safe.

I live in a state of constant overflow of abundance. I am loved at all times. I am open and ready to receive miracles.

I choose to be happy. I am precious. I acknowledge my self-worth. I love my body. I value myself. I radiate and attract love.

I welcome success. I am full of life. I accept and acknowledge my emotions and feelings.

I am aligned with my higher consciousness. I nourish my body with healthy food and my mind with healthy thoughts. I am in charge of how I feel.

I let go of feelings and thoughts that no longer serve a purpose to me. I am free of self-doubt. I have the power to change.

I forgive myself and everyone around me. I am proud of who I am becoming and grateful for who I am.

I am perfect the way I am."

As you repeat these affirmations, feel the truth in your words. Notice any resistance that arises, and gently remind yourself that change takes time. With consistent practice, mirror work helps reprogram your subconscious mind, replacing self-doubt with self-love.

Set a goal to practice mirror work daily for 21 days. Over time, you'll notice shifts in your confidence, mindset, and energy. Mirror work is a testament to the power of aligning with yourself—because when you love and believe in yourself, the Universe follows suit. Use the space below to pen down and personalize your own script. Add affirmations that make you feel good about yourself and repeat them as though you *already* have them. Repetition is the key here.

P.S: When you allow yourself to dream without limits, you're giving your brain permission to explore possibilities you might have otherwise dismissed. You're expanding your vision of what's possible, which in turn expands your actions and outcomes.

"You are limitless."

II
Redefining the Real You

The Universe's secret recipe for turning your dreams into reality starts with a little science magic! Think of it as tuning your mind to the right frequency—when you align your thoughts and beliefs, you literally start attracting the things you want, as if the Universe can't help but hand them over. Now, add a dash of self-concept into the mix, and you've got a powerhouse combo. The way you see yourself directly influences what you pull into your life.

Attracting the life you dream of starts with becoming the version of yourself who's ready to receive it. Because when you feel it, you draw it in. The fastest way to change your life holistically starts with a small change—how you see yourself.

These raw, internal narratives shape our perception of our limits, capabilities, possibilities, and potential. They determine whether we have the confidence to chase and fulfill our dreams or are stunted by self-doubt.

Consider this mental framework a prism through which you can see the world around you. Every thought, emotion, decision, and interaction is shaped by this framework. It's not just about who you are today but also about who you believe you can become.

When you shift this perspective—when you start seeing yourself in a new light—everything around you begins to change. It's like flipping a switch that illuminates a path you couldn't see before.

Manifestation starts when you attract things only when they align with your beliefs and identity. For example, if you see yourself as this confident individual who is capable of deserving at all times, you will automatically attract situations and outcomes that resonate with these traits.

Conversely, if your self-concept is clouded by doubt, fear, insecurity and scarcity, you are standing on the way to wholesome abundance in your life.

This chapter will help you delve deeper into the way you look at yourself and explore answers to how shifting your internal identity will unlock the true potential of manifestation. This concept goes hand in hand with another beautiful concept called self-love, which we will unfold in Chapter 3 of this book.

WHAT'S HOLDING YOU BACK?

Let's move on to an activity that will help you tap into your current self-concept. First, it is vital to identify the areas where you have flared well and where resistance might be holding you back from manifesting right.

Start by asking yourself these questions:

"Who do I believe I am?"

"What do I think I am worthy of?"

"How do I see myself in relation to my desires?"

"Can I achieve my dreams?"

"Am I deserving of all that I aspire to in my life?"

Are you noticing a pattern in your answers? Are your responses in support of the dreams you wish to manifest? Or do they misalign with your objectives?

By answering these questions, you will be able to spot differences between who you are, who you want to become, what you want from life, and especially what you *don't* want for yourself.

For example, in the above set of questions, let's just assume you have this limiting belief that you are not good enough for some reason. There could be many reasons why a thought or an idea as such has slipped into your mind.

Oftentimes, self-concept emerges in your formative years, as early as in your childhood, and continues evolving throughout life. It could be a past incident that shaped your belief system and tricked your brain into believing so. Some of the thoughts could be:

"I am not good enough",

"Why will anyone befriend me"

"I am not worthy or deserving"

"It's impossible for me to get a good life"

"Nothing works out in my favor"

I want you to stop yourself and rewire how you think about it. Start by creating a new statement that reflects your desired self-concept. Reword these thoughts to:

"I am enough"

"I have all the necessary qualities and attributes to be a good friend"

"I am worthy and deserving"

"I have a fulfilling and amazing life"

"Everything works out for my very best"

Remember to start picking these phrases and treating them as daily affirmations from now on. Continue doing that until these affirmations become a part of your daily routine. We discussed the power of affirmations and mirror talk in the last chapter. Trust the process and be authentic to yourself in this entire journey.

At first, you might feel like you have been caught off guard, but once you start taking these steps, you will no longer be far from your manifestations. Sooner than later, they will start being incorporated into your self-concept.

It's that easy!

The key takeaway from this chapter is to understand that manifesting is less about forcing things to happen in your life and more about becoming the highest version of yourself. The idea is all about *being* rather than *doing*.

SEEING THE SHIFT

The faster you redefine your self-concept, the easier it will be for you to see shifts in your 3D reality. So, how to do it?

To begin with, believe in yourself. Seriously, give yourself the credit you deserve for all your incredible capabilities and skills. You've got so much potential, and it's time to start owning it. Never shy away from a little adventure. Taking risks and stepping out of your comfort zone might feel scary, but that's where the magic happens.

And even if something didn't go as planned, look at it as a learning experience rather than a defining moment. This will bring about a substantial shift in perspective, help liberate positive energy, and open up space for new manifestations to arrive.

Only when your self-concept is rooted in worthiness, assurance, and confidence will you lay the foundation for starting a new journey with yourself. When you embody the belief that you are already worthy of what you wish to seek, the external 3D world will start to align with your newfound self-concept.

Let's get your journal ready. It's time for a quick DIY exercise to put this into practice.

ɞ

DIY EXERCISE

For this exercise, take time out to think about what you truly believe about yourself.

Step 1:

Write 10 things you think are standing in your way of achieving your dreams. Basically, pen down your limiting beliefs. Here's the catch–time yourself to sharp 120 seconds. No less, no more.

The point of this exercise is to get your raw, unfiltered thoughts on this question. Increasing the time limit will allow room for editing, which negates the purpose. Remember to be true to yourself and pinpoint the belief that's creating resistance in your life.

You can also use the space provided here to mention your top 10.

Your time starts now!

1.

2.

3.

4.

5.

6.

7.

8.

9.

10.

Step 2:

Now, rewrite that belief into an empowering one. If your limiting belief was *"I'm not good enough to succeed,"* shift it to *"I am more than capable of achieving success, and I attract opportunities easily."* If it's about money, shift *"Money doesn't come easily"* to *"I am a magnet for abundance, and money flows freely to me."*

Step 3:

Here's where the fun part comes in. For the next hour, act as though your new belief is 100% true. If you've chosen the belief *"I attract money easily,"* spend the next hour embodying that person. You might decide to look at your bank account with a sense of gratitude instead of worry, or you might take an action that reflects financial confidence. We will explore this step in detail in Chapter 12.

Step 4:

To anchor your new belief into reality, take one small action that reflects your new mindset. If your belief is about success, maybe you apply for that job you thought you weren't qualified for. If it's about abundance, maybe you make a generous donation or treat yourself without guilt.

Step 5:

After the hour is up, reflect on how you felt. Did your energy shift? Did you feel more empowered? The goal of this exercise is to help you experience the shift in belief and emotional energy in real, so you can see how aligning with new beliefs can lead to real-life shifts.

The more you practice embodying your new beliefs, the faster you can redefine your self-concept.

P.S: Whenever you feel low, let these self-concept exercises become your safe harbor. Imagine them as tools to gently realign your energy and remind you of your innate power.

By weaving them into your daily life, you'll begin to see how profoundly your self-concept shapes not only your manifestations but your entire reality.

Your thoughts about yourself hold the key to unlocking the life you desire.

"Everything you need is within you."

III

Loving Thyself

Some of you might have this wandering question: what does self-love have to do with manifestation? They are independent entities! While that might seem like the concept initially, they are more intertwined than you might think.

One of the greatest aspects of manifesting is the shift from a state of lack, limiting beliefs, and a perception that you are unworthy to a newfound state of embracing your authentic self and imbibing self-love. The further you distance yourself from self-acceptance and self-love, the harder it becomes to recognize the gifts the Universe has for you.

As we learned in the last chapter, our innate ability to manifest our wishes is deeply linked to how we perceive our self-concept. When we truly love and accept ourselves, we send a powerful message to the Universe that is now open to all the goodness it has to send our way. I think of it as a switch that immediately shifts me from a state of lack to a state of abundance.

The second you turn on this switch, you will notice that something magical starts to slip into your life. You will then recognize your true worth. Just by changing the way you view yourself, you open up to a world of possibilities. Ditch the need for applause from the outside world. You don't need anyone else to validate your worthiness—it's already written all over you.

The moment you stop chasing approval from others, you'll feel the shift. Trust me, it's game-changing. A little self-reflection goes a long way in keeping you aligned with your best self. You're not just growing; you're *glowing*.

This transformation can significantly impact every aspect of your life, from personal to professional happiness. Without self-love, manifestation will seem like a chore that you have to do.

Now, let's really explore how we make this shift happen and start imbuing self-love practices into our daily lives. Doing that is easy only when you bid farewell to the limiting beliefs standing in your way, such as self-doubt, and turn them into self-love.

FOSTERING SELF-LOVE HABITS

First things first, never forget to be kind to yourself. Remember to be easy on yourself at all times, especially when things don't go as planned. Only when you are genuinely kind and compassionate to yourself will your perception of the world around you change. Embrace your imperfections with a smile.

Next, learn the subtle art of saying no. It's okay to say "*no*" to the things you don't want to be a part of. Demarcate boundaries from the get-go, and don't succumb to it just out of empathy. There's nothing wrong in saying "*no*" to things that you know will drain your energy or that you are not particularly fond of.

Better yet, find the right set of people. As they say, you are always a combination of the people you hang out with. Start adding more friends into your circle with whom you share your values and who can help make you more productive. Steer away from people who don't appreciate your presence or belittle you. You know you are above it!

Finally, digital detox. It's no secret that social media thrives on a cycle of external validation. From likes to comments, your mood can become tethered to how others perceive you online. Over time, this can erode your sense of self-worth, as your identity becomes a patchwork of others' reactions rather than your own authentic experiences. That's why it's crucial to step back and assess your media consumption. Ask yourself: are these platforms helping you grow, or are they simply feeding into a loop of distraction and self-doubt?

The Internet can indeed be a powerful tool to enhance your skills and broaden your horizons, but it's a double-edged sword. To find balance, start by auditing the apps you spend time on. Identify which ones serve a meaningful purpose in your life—whether they boost your productivity, teach you something new, or connect you to genuine support networks. At the same time, take deliberate steps to distance yourself from apps or platforms that leave you feeling drained, inadequate, or consumed by comparison.

Consider setting specific time limits for social media or designating certain hours of your day as "tech-free." Use this newfound space to reconnect with offline activities that energize and inspire you, like reading, journaling, or spending time with loved ones. The goal isn't to shun technology altogether but to reclaim your power over it.

When you curate your digital habits with intention, you're not just protecting your mental health—you're creating room for authentic joy, growth, and fulfillment.

Know that self-love starts small. Take notes of the things that made you feel good about yourself. It could be something simple like helping a little puppy stuck in your neighborhood, someone complimenting your hair, baking a cake independently, finishing that book you always wanted, or simply starting away from junk food for a week.

Yes, it can be as small as that!

As you accomplish bigger milestones, give yourself a pat on your back. Your confidence level will start shooting up, and in no time, you will feel more empowered, proud, and happy about yourself.

It all starts with you. No one can do this for you. And so is manifestation. One can only manifest for oneself, not for others. On that note, to successfully manifest right, it is crucial to also create a positive environment in and around you. Place yourself amid positivity, and this will hugely exterminate negative influences, fastening your self-love journey.

ෝ

DIY EXERCISE

Sometimes, self-love feels like this big, abstract concept, but trust me—it's simpler than it seems. Let's break it down into something personal, practical, and doable.

Step 1: Spot the Gap

Take a deep breath, relax, and ask yourself this one question: Where am I the hardest on myself?

Think about your day-to-day life. Is it at work, where you feel like you're constantly falling short? Is it your relationships, where you put everyone else first? Or maybe it's the way you see yourself in the mirror? Write it down. Be specific but kind. This isn't about criticizing yourself—it's about gently identifying where you need some love.

Step 2: Imagine the Flip Side

Now that you've pinpointed where you're struggling, picture how you'd treat your best friends if they were in your shoes. What would you say to comfort them? How would you help them feel supported and cared for? Write this down, too—these are the words and actions you're going to offer to yourself from now on.

Step 3: Set a Self-Love Intention

Choose one simple action you can take this week to bring self-love into that area of your life. Here are some examples to get you started:

- If work is your struggle, set boundaries by ending your workday on time, even if your to-do list isn't perfect.
- If relationships feel draining, practice saying "no" to one thing this week without guilt.
- If it's body image, replace one critical thought with a compliment every morning in the mirror.

Step 4: Create a Gentle Reminder

Now, let's make sure you stick with it. Set a small daily reminder—this could be a sticky note on your desk, a gentle phone alarm, or even a mantra you repeat during your morning coffee. Something like: *"I'm worthy of love and care, just as I am."*

Step 5: Reflect and Celebrate

At the end of the week, take 5 minutes to reflect on how this small act of self-love felt. Did it make a difference? Did it feel awkward (and that's okay too)? Celebrate even the tiniest wins—because every step toward self-love is a step worth cheering for.

P.S: There you have it—a simple, personal way to bring a little more love into your life. Start small, stay consistent.

"You're worth the effort."

BREATHE

IV
Activating the Chakras

Now that we have established a strong foundation by diving into frameworks like self-concept and self-love, let's turn to the deeper realms of manifestation —the space where your mind, spirit, and the energy of the Universe converge. When you as an entity and your mind align perfectly with the synchronicity of the Universe, you begin to let the flow of energy guide your thoughts, actions, and emotions—something we will read more about in Chapter 7 of this book. When you tune into this harmony, your thoughts, actions, and emotions begin to work in seamless alignment with what you truly desire. This idea takes us to the heart of this chapter: the 7 chakras.

Prepare to deepen your understanding of how your inner energy flows, how your mind and manifestation are interrelated and discover how nurturing them will unlock new dimensions of your manifesting abilities.

THE 7 CHAKRAS

The word *Chakra* originates from Sanskrit, meaning *"spinning wheel."* Imagine these as energy centers in your body, continuously spinning and maintaining your life's balance. While the human body is said to have over a hundred chakras, 7 primary ones hold the key to your emotional, physical, and spiritual well-being.

These chakras begin at the base of your spine and flow upward to the crown of your head. Each is associated with a unique color, part of the body, mantra, and natural element. When these chakras are open and aligned, your energy flows freely, and you operate at your best—both emotionally and physically.

Though invisible to the eye and intangible to the touch, these 7 chakras serve as a sacred blueprint for your personal well-being. Each chakra is deeply connected to the natural elements around us. The first 5 chakras resonate with the physical forces of Earth, Water, Fire, Air, and Space, grounding us to the tangible world. Meanwhile, the final 2 chakras transcend the physical, aligning with the ethereal energies of Light and Cosmic Consciousness, guiding us toward higher realms of existence. Together, they form a harmonious flow between the body, mind, and spirit.

Once you understand the relevance of each element with its chakra, you should be able to sense how that element manifests within your body. Viewing your body through these symbolic lenses can unlock new reservoirs of energy.

Let's take a closer look at the 7 chakras, one by one:

Muladhara Chakra (Root Chakra)

- Location: Base of the spine (pelvic floor)
- Seed mantra: Lam
- Color: Red
- Element: Earth
- Yoga pose: Tree pose (Vrikshasana)
- Symbol: A four-petaled lotus

The root chakra located at your pelvic floor governs our family ties, belongingness and guardedness. This is the realm of our instinctual urges around food, sleep, and survival. It is also where our ability to be afraid and avoid, stems from.

When this chakra is perfectly balanced, you will exhibit emotions of survival, stability, ambition, and self-sufficiency. When blocked, malnourished, or imbalanced, you exhibit behaviors of low self-esteem, need, and lack of confidence. To nurture this chakra, engage in grounding practices like walking barefoot on grass or practicing stability-focused yoga poses.

Svadhishthana Chakra (Sacral Chakra)

- Location: Lower abdomen
- Seed mantra: Vam
- Color: Orange
- Element: Water
- Yoga poses: Triangle pose (Trikonasana), Goddess pose (Deviasana)
- Symbol: A six-petaled lotus

The sacral chakra represents the life cycles of birth, death, and rebirth. As it represents the reproductive organs, it represents fluidity, creativity, and fertility.

When this chakra is in balance, you feel vibrant, compassionate, and inspired, with a natural receptiveness to change. When blocked, malnourished, or imbalanced, you can feel emotionally explosive, uninspired, irritable, and lacking focus or creativity. You can rekindle this energy through art, writing your thoughts out, or any other creative form of expression.

Manipura Chakra (Solar Plexus Chakra)

- Location: Navel region
- Seed mantra: Ram
- Color: Yellow
- Element: Fire
- Yoga poses: Boat pose (Navasana), Cobra pose (Bhujangasana), Forward bend pose (Paschimottanasana)
- Symbol: A ten-petaled lotus

This energy center is associated with the digestive system and is thus driven by the elements of fire, purpose, and individual power. This chakra is dubbed as the powerhouse of your body.

When balanced, one feels energetic, confident, and vivacious. You tend to become more productive and strive to get things done without procrastinating or hovering. When this energy center is out of sync, one can experience physical issues such as liver problems, digestive ailments, and even diabetes. On an emotional level, you might struggle with anger and depression and lose your temper over trivial things. Strengthen this chakra by practicing fire breathing (Kapalabhati Pranayama) or engaging in self-empowering affirmations.

Anahata Chakra (Heart Chakra)

- Location: Heart or chest region
- Seed mantra: Yam
- Color: Green
- Element: Air
- Yoga poses: Camel pose (Ustrasana), Fish pose (Matsyasana), Bridge pose (Ardha Setubandhasana)
- Symbol: A 12-petaled lotus flower

The heart chakra is said to be the central point for your emotions. It is the center that can radiate your highest emotions, such as unconditional love, faith, passion, and security, while at the same time, it is also the bed where you find your deepest feelings of loneliness, disappointment, despair, and unhappiness.

When balanced, you exude optimism, compassion, and the ability to form healthy, meaningful relationships. When blocked, you feel anxious, fearful, and angry all the time. You may also fear rejection and might form dysfunctional relationships. To heal from past emotional wounds and foster healthier relationships, focus on opening your heart chakra through practices like self-love affirmations, deep breathing exercises, or heart-opening yoga poses.

Vishuddha Chakra (Throat Chakra)

- Location: Throat region
- Seed mantra: Ham
- Color: Blue
- Element: Space
- Yoga poses: Shoulderstand (Salamba Sarvangasana), Plough pose (Halasana)
- Symbol: A 16-petaled lotus flower

On a physical level, the throat is the home of speech and hearing. On a spiritual level, this center is all about expanding our conversation to the divine force.

When balanced, you find it easy to communicate your emotions in healthy ways. When blocked, you might often feel like you can't find your voice or are afraid to speak the truth. You find it difficult to let the person in front of you know how you feel on the inside. You suppress your voice and opinion. To nurture this chakra, engage in chanting, journaling, or practicing yoga poses that stretch the neck and throat.

Ajna Chakra (Third Eye Chakra)

- Location: Between the eyebrows (the midpoint of the forehead)
- Seed mantra: Om
- Color: Indigo
- Element: Light
- Yoga poses: Easy pose (Sukhasana), Headstand (Shirshasana)

- Symbol: An inverted triangle within a circle, flanked by two lotus petals

Located between the eyebrows, this point is also said to be the third eye. It is used as the focal point to develop more concentration and awareness. Meditating upon this chakra is said to help increase concentration, intuition, and insight.

When balanced, one does not show attachment to material things and feels more content emotionally and spiritually. When imbalanced, one can cause physical problems like headaches, blurry vision, and constant eye strain. To activate this chakra, focus on mindfulness, visualization, and meditative practices aimed at improving concentration and intuition.

Sahastrara Chakra (Crown Chakra)

- Location: Crown of the head
- Seed mantra: Om
- Color: White
- Element: Cosmic energy
- Yoga pose: Corpse pose (Savasana)
- Symbol: A thousand-petaled lotus surrounding an inverted triangle

The final chakra centers on spirituality, enlightenment, and dynamic thought and energy. It allows for the inward flow of wisdom and gives the gift of cosmic consciousness. This is the center from which you connect to the point beyond the spiritual realm.

When balanced, you feel enlightened and experience greater joy in life. This is also where you see points like duality, conflict, and separation erased. When not balanced, you don't feel connected with divine consciousness. You also have a constant sense of frustration and invite destructive feelings. To align this chakra, engage in meditative silence, gratitude practices, or visualizations of white light flowing through the crown of your head.

DIY EXERCISE

So, how do we activate these chakras?

By meditating and visualizing each chakra by following these steps:

Step 1:

Find a distraction-free area and shut yourself away from noises, social media, and your phone. Ensure that you are not disturbed for the next 10 minutes.

Step 2:

Find a comfortable place. It can be on the floor, on a mat, or in a chair. Ideally, it is advised to sit on the ground. You are free to choose your space.

Step 3:

Cross your legs and place your arms on the top of your knees. Close your eyes and lower your gaze. Yes, it is possible to do that.

Step 4:
With what we just learned, start with the root chakra, visualize the symbol and color, and chant the mantra for at least one minute. Visualize a red, four-petalled lotus flower rotating in a clockwise direction at the base of your spine. Now, continue doing so for the other 6 chakras. You can start with one minute of meditation and visualization per chakra, and with time, you can try to achieve 5 minutes per chakra.

Personally, I try to keep a count of meditating for exactly 28 minutes every day, spending 4 minutes per chakra. Alternatively, you can tune into many guided audios for chakra meditation on YouTube. Once, you are through the chants, try also adding the yoga asanas into your daily routine. I have been doing this for a while now, and the effects have been profound.

I battled high with the Throat and Heart chakras. Both of these chakras were blocked. I started inculcating chants, visualization, and meditation into my daily routine, and I almost started to look at life from a different perspective altogether. It helped me colossally change the way I look at life. That's why I wanted to add this to my book so that all my readers can reap its benefits. Speaking of meditation, let's now deep-dive into how to meditate the right way and why it is a must-add part of your daily routine.

P.S: Unblocking chakras is not about achieving perfection but embracing the beauty of growth and healing. With each step, you're aligning closer to your true self.

"Go shine your light on the world."

V
Mindful Awakening

Meditation isn't just about sitting cross-legged in a candlelit room, hoping your mind doesn't wander to your grocery list. It's much deeper than that.

It's like discovering a secret door to your own mind—one that leads to clarity, calm, and a spark of magic in your everyday life. It's the ultimate tool for navigating life's chaos with a quiet kind of confidence. For me, it has always been a journey inward, a journey nothing short of transformational. Think of it as a calm lake, undisturbed by ripples, reflecting everything around it with clarity. This is what meditation does for the mind; it helps us reconnect with ourselves, find focus, and unlock untapped potential.

In this chapter, we'll explore how meditation transcends being a spiritual or wellness practice, becoming a powerful tool for cultivating self-awareness, enhancing mental clarity, and even aligning ourselves with our goals. Whether you're a beginner or someone seeking to deepen your practice, this chapter will provide practical insights, techniques, and inspiration to help you embrace the transformative power of meditation.

For over a year, I have disciplined myself enough to silence the mental buzz in my head for just 15 minutes every day. It wasn't easy at first. My thoughts were like unruly toddlers, running wild and demanding attention. But over time, it helped me fade the noise within, the clutter within. It significantly reduced my stream of thoughts, and I discovered a version of myself I didn't even know existed—calmer, more focused, and deeply in tune with my intuition.

You know how they say, *"Trust your gut"*? Well, meditation taught me how to actually *listen* to mine. You can manifest right only when you have mastered the underrated art of listening to your intuitions. When you do that, you create a safe space for your minds to be raw, uninhibited, and free of judgment. In a way, you open yourself to a sea of possibilities.

THE INNER SANCTUARY

In my last book, and even here, you have often found me harping on how our thoughts and beliefs create our reality. And whether you find that hard to digest, that is how it works. If you don't believe you are truly capable of something, you tend to put yourself out of the situation or simply give in trying.

That's where affirmations come in. Pair them with meditation, add positive sentences and believe in your ability and worthiness—you've got a recipe for pure magic. While meditating, truly feel and visualize as though whatever you want to manifest has arrived, and that's when you'll step into your inner sanctuary, where you find peace through meditation.

For instance, if you truly think you should be winning the next *"Employee of the Month"* award, start affirming to your routine. Such as,

"I deserve to be awarded with the "Employee of the Month" award."

"I am sincere, devoted to my job, and maintain healthy, professional relationships with all my colleagues."

"I know I have all that it takes to bag this recognition."

"I am worthy."

Say them like you *mean* it. Picture the applause, the pride on your boss's face, the celebratory win with your colleagues. When you are certain about your worth or purpose, people sense it, too. Engrain yourself with a mantra, *"Everything works out in my favor,"* and I say this from my personal experience: things do start to look up. This is more like a message that you are signaling to the Universe that you are now open to receiving all that it has to give you.

It's not just about words; it's about energy. This shift in energy is all you need to kickstart your manifestation from meditating. When you radiate belief in yourself, it reflects that energy right back to you.

Also, full disclaimer: do not pressure yourself to imbue this activity right away into your schedule. You don't even have to meditate for 2 hours straight. Listen to your intuition and pay attention to what your body demands.

It took me a while, too, to inculcate this habit and pursue it diligently for a year now. I started small with just 5 minutes of meditation. Over time, those 5 minutes turned into 10, then 15. Now, it's a non-negotiable part of my day. And honestly? I wish someone had nudged me to start earlier.

Luckily, you have this book!

Consider this book a sign from the Universe that it's time to become your highest self!

RECALIBRATING FOR TRANSFORMATION

It's simple—when you meditate, you raise your vibrational frequency. That's a fancy way of saying you feel good—like, *really* good. And when you feel good, you attract good things. It's like sending the Universe a text that says, *"I'm ready for all the amazing stuff you've got for me!"* When you ask anything of the Universe with an elevated vibration and energy, it is easier to attract what you have manifested.

But that's not all.

Tapping into your subconscious mind allows you to tune into your inner thoughts and transform into a state of being more aware of the limiting beliefs that need to be erased. It clears out the clutter—self-doubt, negativity, fear—and makes space for clarity, focus, and creativity. Suddenly, you're not just reacting to life; you're creating it.

And let's not forget the ultimate benefit, *peace.* The whole point of meditation is to fasten your reach to inner tranquility. By quieting the constant noise inside your head, you can now clearly focus on what you want to manifest, thereby removing specks of doubt, fear, and negative thinking that would have blocked your manifestation from coming true anyway. We will zoom more into this in

Chapter 10. For now, let me share an experience that happened to me recently. I dub it a *"Soul leaving my body"* experience.

Even though I don't want to scare my readers, I have to share this supernatural experience that did happen to me.

THE EXPERIENCE

"As I sat in my meditation, I closed my eyes. The room around me faded into the background, entering that familiar, quiet space within myself. I'm breathing deeply, visualizing my dreams as if they were already real and as though I'm actually living them in reality. As I was slowly slipping into a deeper state, something extraordinary happened. I was taken to a state that was utterly indescribable yet so real it left me shaken. I had simply surrendered to the meditation, and it took me somewhere beyond what I had ever experienced before.

Mental images began flashing through my mind, vivid and clear, almost as if they were memories instead of dreams. I wasn't just visualizing anymore; I was there. I saw myself traveling to breathtaking places, lands I had always dreamed of visiting but hadn't yet touched in reality. I was standing before the Eiffel Tower, the air crisp and alive with the sound of Paris. My partner was beside me, holding my hand, our eyes meeting in a shared moment of wonder.

Then the scene shifted—I was in a delivery room. The soft cries of our newborn filled the space, and my partner stood right there beside me, tears of joy glistening in his eyes. I was experiencing the fullness of life, not as some distant possibility but as my reality. And suddenly—time ceased to exist. It was a void—a vast, endless void of pure stillness. I was suspended in a place where there was no past, future, or even present. No form, no boundaries. I had entered a space where nothing mattered, but everything existed, leaving only a deep, infinite stillness. Just an overwhelming sense of peace that was so profound, it took my breath away. I was transfixed.

And in that nothingness, I felt a presence. A divine force. It was as if I was no longer alone in that room. It was as if the Universe, or whatever higher power exists, was standing watch over me. It didn't speak, but I felt its silent message, "I'm here for you. You are not alone."

The feeling was so powerful, like being held by a loving parent who, while letting their child explore the vastness of the ocean, gently calls them back when they've gone too far. And just as easily, I felt this 3D world we live in—began to call me back. It was subtle at first, like a faint tug on the edge of my consciousness, but it grew stronger, pulling me back to the room, to the present moment. It was as if life itself was summoning me, reminding me that I was still tethered to this physical world, no matter how far I had ventured beyond it.

When I finally opened my eyes, it was as if I had crossed back through a veil, and I found myself sitting in the very same room I had started in, but everything was different. I was different. My breath was shallow, and I had goosebumps all over my skin. I felt like I had just touched something divine—something that goes beyond our everyday experience of life. And the truth of it washed over me like a wave—I was there. It happened."

Meditation had taken me to a place I never knew existed—a space where desires, time, and physical form blur into one infinite canvas. It wasn't just a mental exercise; it was a powerful, tangible experience.

This is what meditation is capable of: taking you beyond your thoughts and into a realm where your deepest desires are already real and where the divine calms you.

I'll now share one of the most amazing meditating techniques I have used in my personal growth and this will help you too.

&

DIY EXERCISE

This meditation technique is called a "Body Scan." It will immensely help you release tension, increase awareness, and become more present. Plus, it will help clear energy blocks that stand in the way of your manifestation. Follow these easy steps:

Step 1: Find a Quiet Space

Sit or lie down in a comfortable position in a quiet environment. Close your eyes and take a few deep breaths to center yourself.

Step 2: Focusing on Your Breath

Breathe deeply and naturally. As you inhale, imagine that you're breathing in calm, healing energy. As you exhale, release any tension or stress. With every breath you take, bring in awareness.

Step 3: Bring in Awareness

Start by bringing your awareness to your feet. Are they warm, cold, tense, or relaxed? Take a moment to acknowledge and breathe into that part of your body. Move upward. Gradually move your awareness up your body, from your feet to your ankles, then to your calves, knees, and thighs. Continue releasing tension and move to the core.

Bring attention to your lower abdomen, pelvis, and lower back. And then to your chest and heart. Feel the rise and fall of your chest as you breathe. Focus on your heart center, where your emotional energy resides. As you exhale, imagine releasing any emotional tension stored in this area, especially any doubts, fears, or negative emotions that could be blocking your manifestation.

Next, shift your awareness to your shoulders, arms, and hands. Shoulders often carry stress, so consciously relax them with each breath. Let go of any burden or weight you're holding. Move your attention to your neck, face, and head. Soften your facial muscles, particularly your forehead and jaw, which often hold tension. Imagine the top of your head as a connection point with the Universe, receiving energy and clarity.

Now, what if your mind wanders during meditation? I want you to know that that's perfectly normal and natural, don't worry. Instead of resisting those thoughts or judging yourself, approach them with curiosity and acceptance. Picture each thought as a leaf floating down a stream; notice it, acknowledge it, and let it drift away without clinging to it. Bring your focus back to your breath. The goal isn't to force your mind into silence but to gently guide it back whenever it strays. Over time, this practice strengthens your ability to stay present while cultivating patience and self-compassion.

Once you've scanned each part of your body, bring your awareness to your whole body as a unified field of energy. Feel the lightness and relaxation flowing through you. Visualize yourself glowing with positive energy, aligned and ready to receive your desires.

As you finish the body scan, take a moment to mentally affirm your desires. For example, *"I am open and ready to receive abundance."* Then, let go and trust that the Universe is working with you.

P.S: Mindful meditation is incomplete without learning the know-how of the right kind of breathwork to practice. Breathwork brings structure and depth to mindfulness. It's the rhythmic pulse that keeps you steady amidst the chaos. Different techniques can elicit vastly different outcomes, from calming an anxious mind to energizing your body on a sluggish day. But how do you know which type of breathwork aligns with your goals? What is the "right" kind for your practice? Get ready to zoom into that in the next chapter and know its true essence.

"You are worthy!"

VI

A Hidden Superpower

Isn't it fascinating how we often overlook the most vital part of being alive? Breathing.

Yes! We do that seemingly simple, automatic act non-stop without even thinking about it. I think of breath to be so much more than a life-sustaining reflex. A gateway. A tool. A power source that can unlock your body's hidden energy, heal emotional wounds, and align you with the vast, infinite Universe.

Breathing isn't just about oxygen and carbon dioxide—it's about connection. When you breathe mindfully, you align yourself with the heartbeat of nature. It's like tuning into a cosmic radio station that whispers:

"You are infinite."

"You are capable."

"You are worthy."

Through conscious breathwork, you can supercharge your manifestation journey, transforming desires into reality with clarity and purpose. This chapter dives headfirst into the powerful relationship between breath and manifestation. Think of the breath as your personal magic wand, amplifying your energy and sending crystal-clear signals to the Universe. When combined with focused intention, breath can magically amplify our energetic output, signaling the Universe that we are ready to receive.

Ready to tap into that magic? Let's go.

A MODERN TAKE

Breathwork is an ancient art rooted in cultures that have been exploring its magic for thousands of years. Let's take a journey back; in the ancient yogic traditions of India, breath control—or *Pranayama*—was a cornerstone of spiritual practice. *Prana* means life force, and *Ayama* translates to extension. Together, it means the conscious extension of life itself.

Today, science is catching up to what these traditions knew all along. Studies show that breathwork has been the single most vital tool to induce personal growth, think clearer, reduce trauma-induced depression, increase oxygen flow to the brain, and even rewire your nervous system.

Plus, it is through breathwork that you can truly pay attention to what your body has to say, become more aware and tap into one's consciousness. More concretely, it leads to a better sleep pattern, better mood, away from the whimsical swings, enhanced emotional and spiritual well-being, and reduced anxiety.

Inculcating habitual breathwork can be a miracle cure as our breath holds the power to unlock mental clarity, emotional healing, and physical rejuvenation. What I like most about this process—it's free, and you already have everything you need to start.

INHALE, EXHALE

Let's now explore how breathwork and manifestation are related and how the former fuels the latter. As we learned in Chapter 5, the right meditation opens the doors to seamless manifestation. Similarly, breathwork is a crucial element that makes meditation a total game-changer.

Are you holding on to tension, anxiety, or unresolved emotions in your body? That's like having a boulder in the middle of your stream of energy. They create energetic blocks that make it difficult for you to attract what you desire. Deep, conscious breathing clears that boulder, creating a free-flowing river for your dreams to manifest.

Breathwork is a way to release tension and create space for new, aligned energy to flow. A higher vibrational state allows you to feel good, and when you feel good, you align with the vibration of your desires. By consciously using the breath to raise your vibration, you become an energetic match for what you manifest, thereby matching your vibrational state. Anchor manifestations in the subconscious by pairing breathwork with visualization or affirmations, where your breath becomes the carrier of your intention. With each inhalation, you actively draw in your desires, and with each exhalation, you release doubts, fears, and attachments that might be holding you back. This rhythmic cycle doesn't just feel good; it rewires your subconscious to *believe* that your dreams are already on their way. And belief, my friend, is half the battle.

THE RITUAL

Adding breathwork to your daily routine is like discovering a cheat code for life. Start small. In the morning, before you even check your phone, sit quietly and take a few deep breaths. As you inhale, imagine yourself soaking up positivity, and as you exhale, let go of yesterday's stress.

I've found that breaking my day into smaller, intentional moments of breathwork creates a profound sense of alignment and peace.

In the mornings, before the world starts pulling me in every direction, I dedicate a few quiet minutes to a simple breathwork practice. As I inhale deeply, I set the tone for the day, embracing positivity and welcoming the opportunities ahead.

Around midday, when the inevitable stress or distractions slip in, I pause again. These moments of calming breathwork feel like a reset button, helping me realign with my higher self and refocus on what truly matters.

In the evening, as the day winds down, I practice deep, deliberate breathing while visualizing my desires as already fulfilled. I see them vividly in my mind's eye, creating a powerful imprint on my subconscious before sleep. These daily practices, though brief, have become a grounding force, reminding me that growth is a journey. This doesn't just feel calming—it feels transformative.

Remember to go easy on yourself. You don't have to meditate thrice a day if you don't feel like it. This book is a journey to help you transform into your highest self and grow as an individual. You can definitely set your pace and do as your body craves. Having said that, try to inculcate it at least once a day at a specific time of your choice—morning–noon, or late evening before hitting the bed. Now, let's get you some practical breathwork exercises that can reset you.

ॐ

DIY EXERCISE

In my last book, I already discussed the *"Box Breathing Technique."* You can add that to your routine or even explore new ones as prescribed for this exercise.

If we go over traditional forms of ancient breathwork techniques, I can't miss the *"Pranayama"* breathing technique from the list. Regular practice of *Pranayama* can help us gain greater control over our physical and mental health. This set of breathing exercises aims to connect our body and mind and promote mindfulness. For the DIY exercise today, we shall learn a timeless technique called *"Anulom Vilom"*, or alternate nostril breathing. If you haven't practiced it ever, or it's been a hot minute, here are the steps to follow along:

Step 1: Sit down with your legs crossed.

Step 2: Place your left hand on your left knee and lift your right hand up to your nose.

Step 3: Breathe out, then close your right nostril with your right thumb.

Step 4: Breathe in through your left nostril, then use your fingers to close it.

Step 5: Release your thumb from your right nostril and breathe out through this side.

Step 6: Breathe in through your right nostril, then close it again with your thumb.

Step 7: Release your fingers from your left nostril and breathe out through this side. You've now completed a full cycle.

Step 8: Repeat as much as desired, being sure to end on a completed cycle.

As you practice these breathwork techniques, know that the power of your breath is always with you. It's your secret weapon for shifting your energy, clearing blocks, and becoming an unstoppable force of manifestation. Pair it with meditation, affirmations, and inspired action, and you're no longer just dreaming—you're *creating*.

As you practice these breathwork techniques, remember that your breath is more than just a tool—it's your constant companion, your invisible ally, and your secret superpower. The power of your breath is always with you, waiting to be tapped into whenever you need it. Whether it's to calm the storm of anxiety, ignite a spark of creativity, or reset your focus, your breath is the ultimate key to transformation. It's not just about breathing to survive; it's about breathing to thrive.

Does adding the right course of meditation and breathwork enough to nudge the needle in your favor? You also need to take the right course of action, or better yet, inspired actions, and then add the right set of habits that will allow you to cooperate with the Universe. Let's unravel all that in the next part.

P.S: Breathe deeply, set your intentions, and watch as your manifestations come to life effortlessly.

"Breathe. Believe. Become"

BALANCE

VII

Action Meets
Intuition

I've come to this realization that the easiest route to manifestation is to send out a crystal-clear signal to the Universe and back it up with action. Yes, action. That's the catch—but don't let it scare you. This isn't about grinding endlessly. It's about alignment, intention, and flow.

We've all had moments when we dream big and imagine ourselves living the life we've always wanted. A life where your goals feel within reach, and every step feels destined? Simply, wishing and waiting won't get you there. But acting in harmony with your vision will. You need to act and, more importantly, act in *alignment* with your vision.

When there's a pull, a magnetic force inside you—a fiery urge nudging you toward something meaningful. That's not random; that's your inner compass. When you follow that pull, you're aligning yourself with a universal flow.

It's not random. You're taking deliberate, meaningful steps, not just checking off to-do lists. More like a powerful declaration that you're ready to transform your thoughts into things.

But here's the secret ingredient—that intention must be followed by a genuine, burning desire from within to take the right course of action. That's how you truly ignite the process of manifestation. Every action you take becomes a signal, a ripple that flows out into the Universe, echoing back with opportunities and synchronicities that align with your desires.

When you pursue a dream with passion, it's as if the Universe begins to rearrange itself to support you. It's like the Universe is saying,

"Okay, I hear you, now let's see how you can get there!"

That brings us to understand a concept called "Inspired action" and how is it different from "Forced action."

DISSECTING THE DIFFERENCES

Inspired action flows naturally. It's when you feel pulled toward something because it excites you; it feels right. There's a certain lightness to it. Even when it requires effort, there's joy and purpose bubbling underneath. You're not dragging your feet; you're gliding. Ever had a moment where something just *clicked*? It's like your inner guidance system is whispering, *"This way!"* You might feel a surge of excitement or even a sense of calm assurance that you're on the right path. It doesn't feel like work, and though it might still require effort, the energy behind it feels light and positive. These actions are in sync with your intentions, and they come naturally as you follow the breadcrumbs of life. You're not forcing them; instead, they feel like a natural next step toward your goal. That's inspired action!

Forced action, on the other hand, feels heavy. It's when you push yourself to do something because you think you *have* to, not because you truly want to. There's resistance, a lack of joy, and often, frustration. It's when you work hard, but it's a grind. You're taking steps, but they don't feel aligned. It's riddled with doubt, frustration, and resistance. When you're forcing something, it feels off, as if you're swimming against the current. Sure, you're taking steps, but they don't lead anywhere fulfilling.

Ever tried forcing yourself to finish a task just because it's on your to-do list, even though your heart isn't in it? That action is forced, and it rarely leads to anything fulfilling. The reason you should follow inspired action over forced action is simple—it's more effective.

When you're inspired, you're connected to the energy of your desires, and that energy creates a multiplier effect. You're not just ticking off tasks; you're moving purposefully, and the Universe responds in kind. Doors open. Things fall into place. And you find yourself making progress almost effortlessly.

SPOT THE SPARK

How to spot an inspired action when it comes your way? It starts with tuning in to your inner guidance system—your intuition. It has all the answers. Pay attention to those little nudges, the sudden insights, or the spark of excitement that lights you up. That's your spiritual GPS saying, *"Go for it!"*

Let's say you've been dreaming of starting your own business. You've set the intention, you've envisioned what it looks like, and then, out of nowhere, you meet someone at a party who has experience in the very industry you're interested in.

That's a signal!

It's the Universe giving you a nudge to take the next step. It might seem small, but these are the moments that lead to bigger opportunities.

Inspired ideas often sneak up on you. It might show up as a sudden thought, a gut feeling, or even through a conversation or something you read. It feels right—not in a logical way, but in an intuitive sense. There's excitement and you'll feel a burst of energy or enthusiasm toward the idea.

Start paying attention to these moments. When you feel a spark, follow that spark! Give it some space to grow in your mind. The more you tune in, the easier it becomes to recognize when the Universe is nudging you forward. The key is to follow that spark with the first step, however small.

Taking the first step doesn't have to be monumental. In fact, trust your gut, your intuition. Often, we second-guess ourselves, letting fear or overthinking block the flow. The more you learn to recognize that feeling of inspiration, the easier it becomes to confidently move forward. Start with the small steps. Send that email, make that phone call, or take that class. Whatever the idea is, act on it without overanalyzing. Remember, inspired actions often feel like "next logical steps" rather than giant leaps. Think of it like dipping your toes in the water to test it.

And you might not have all the answers right away, and that's okay. The path will reveal itself as you move forward.

TUNE INTO INTUITION

Taking inspired action starts with being in tune with your inner guidance. This means quieting the noise around you and listening intently to what's within. Meditation, journaling, and simply spending time alone in reflection can help you tap into your inner voice. The more connected you are, the clearer your next steps will be.

Step 1: Act Now, Not Later

Once you get that nudge, take action immediately. Procrastination is the enemy of inspiration. The longer you wait, the more that initial excitement fades. Act while the energy is fresh. Remember, the first step doesn't have to be huge—it just has to be taken.

Step 2: Listen to Your Body

Your body is an excellent guide when it comes to inspired action. Notice how you feel when thinking about an idea or opportunity. Does your body feel light and open, or does it feel tense and heavy? That's a clue!

Step 3: Follow Your Joy

If something excites you or lights you up, that's your sign! When joy is present, it's a powerful indicator that you're in alignment with your desires. Pay attention to what feels good—this is the Universe showing you your path.

Step 4: Embrace the Journey

Inspired action is not always about the end result. Sometimes, it's about the journey itself. Be open to the idea that the steps you're taking might lead you in unexpected directions.

Step 5: Practice Consistently

Manifestation isn't about one big leap; it's about consistent, inspired action. Small, inspired steps taken over time compound into big results. Stay consistent, even if progress feels slow at times. Know that every action you take is building momentum. Trust that each step, no matter how small or seemingly insignificant, is guiding you closer to your ultimate goal.

∞

DIY EXERCISE

Alright! It looks like we haven't seen your journal in a while. It's time to take it out from the dusty cupboard and use it for this DIY exercise. Alternatively, you may also use the space provided here for this activity.

Let's start with setting an intention today.

Before starting your next day, set an intention that you will stick to for a day. Ask yourself: what is one inspired action I can take today to move closer to my goal? It doesn't have to be big, but it should feel right. Time yourself for not more than 5 minutes.

For example, if you are looking for newer freelance opportunities, you can perhaps reach out to 10 leads on LinkedIn or check in with your past clients to see if they require your services. It can also be something small, like drinking 3 liters of water daily. Of late, you have been forgetting to drink water more often than not, and you want to return to your healthier self.

What's your intended action for the day?

Now, throughout your day, pay attention to the little nudges you feel. When something sparks your interest, take note. It could be a thought, an idea, or a feeling that urges you to act. The moment you feel inspired to do something, even if it's small, do it. Write these in your journal and track how often they show up. You'll be surprised at how frequently inspiration strikes when you're open to it.

And finally, before ending your day, take 5 minutes to reflect. Ask yourself:

What inspired action did I take today? How did it feel?

Reflecting on your actions will help you stay aligned and keep you focused on the progress you're making, even if it's subtle. Over time, you'll notice how these small, inspired steps lead you closer to your bigger goals.

P.S: This simple routine—setting an intention, following through on nudges, and reflecting—helps you stay in tune with your inner guidance and ensures you consistently take inspired action in your daily life.

"Step boldly into your future."

VIII
Everyday Alignments

Have you ever stopped to think about how the tiny things you do every day quietly shape your life? It's like laying bricks to build a castle. At first, it doesn't look like much—a single brick here, another there—but before you know it, you're standing in front of something extraordinary.

That's how habits work.

They're not just things you *do*. They are like the bricks that build the foundation of your life. They're the DNA of who you are, at our core—every choice, every action you repeat day after day, gradually molds you into the person you become.

When we talk about manifestation and spirituality, there's often a misconception that you simply think positively, and voila, your desires show up! What no one reveals is—that you becoming your "highest self"—that version of you that's fully aligned with your dreams, values, and potential—doesn't happen overnight.

No one wakes up one morning and suddenly has it all together. It's not about grand gestures or life-changing epiphanies. It's about the little things. The tiny, seemingly insignificant actions you choose daily are the ones that steer your life in new directions.

Manifestation works hand-in-hand with action, and habits are the key. Habits instill discipline, and that discipline helps you align with your higher self, the version of you who already has everything you desire.

Discipline is the driving force behind this transformation. Think of it as the bridge between where you are now and where you want to be.

When you commit to a habit, you're telling yourself (and the Universe) that you're serious about your growth. It's like sending a message out that says, *"I'm ready to take control of my life."*

HABITS OF POWERFUL MANIFESTORS

Creating and sticking to habits helps you become a better version of yourself and aligns you with your highest self. That's the version of you who lives in your vision of the future.

It's the "you" that already has the career, the relationships, the health, the abundance, and the happiness you're working toward. When you adopt the habits that your future self would have, you're essentially stepping into that version of yourself today.

For example, imagine your highest self as someone who is calm, collected, and at peace. How would they start their day?

Maybe with a morning meditation or journaling session. Imagine them as someone who's physically fit and energetic. What habits would they have? Probably regular exercise, a balanced diet, and daily movement. The habits you choose to implement are a direct reflection of the future you're creating.

And here's the beauty of it: these habits don't have to be monumental changes. They can be small, almost insignificant shifts that, when repeated over time, create incredible results.

THE RIPPLE EFFECT

Let's dive into the magic of small habits. Have you ever thrown a pebble into a pond and watched how the ripples grow, getting larger and larger? That's exactly how small habits work. When done consistently, they create a ripple effect that extends far beyond the initial action.

Take something as simple as drinking a glass of water first thing in the morning. It's a small act, but over time, it becomes a powerful part of your day. You start to feel more hydrated, more alert, and energized. You might then find yourself more motivated to take a short walk or prepare a healthy breakfast.

That small act of hydration sets off a chain reaction that impacts your physical health, your mood, and, eventually, your productivity.

When you start feeling better physically, your mental and emotional well-being follows, leading to a clearer, more focused mind that's ready to manifest your dreams.

As I mentioned earlier in this book, meditation was a big deal for me personally. I always wondered how monks go on meditating for longer periods when it was difficult to quiet my mind for just 5 minutes! Therefore, I started small. I committed to just 10 minutes each morning.

At first, I was able to convince myself, *"It seems minor, right?"* But over time, those 10 minutes helped me feel calmer, more focused, and strangely energized, like I'd hit reset on my brain. The more consistent I became, the more those 10 minutes began to ripple out into other areas of my life.

That's the power of small habits—their effect multiplies over time. It's not about making huge, sweeping changes overnight. It's about taking small, intentional steps every single day. Over time, these small habits build up to significant shifts in your life.

MANIFESTATION TOOLBOX

If you're wondering what habits to incorporate into your daily routine to help you manifest more effectively, don't worry—there are some must-add practices that can bring you closer to your dreams.

The best part? These habits are simple, easy to implement, and won't take up hours of your day. Yet, when done regularly, they create profound shifts. Here are some habits that will definitely hone you as an individual:

Start journaling. Writing down your thoughts, goals, and desires every day helps solidify them in your mind. It's a way to process emotions, get clarity, and reinforce your intentions. Plus, it's a great way to track your progress and growth over time.

Move your body. This is important.

Movement is key to keeping your energy flowing. Whether it's a morning stretch, yoga, or a quick walk, moving your body shifts stagnant energy and helps you feel more vibrant and alive. When your body feels good, your mind ensues. This habit helps you maintain a positive vibration throughout the day.

Remember to take mindfulness breaks throughout the day. These don't have to be long—just a few minutes where you stop, breathe, and bring yourself back to the present moment.

It's a great way to reset, release stress, and ensure you're not running on autopilot. The more present you are, the more aware you'll be of opportunities and ideas that align with your manifestations.

Want to add a new habit to your routine? Try "habit stacking," where you attach a new habit to something you already do daily. For example, if you want to start practicing gratitude, you could add it to your morning coffee routine. While your coffee brews, jot down 3 things you're grateful for. By linking the new habit to an existing one, you're more likely to stick with it. For example, if you love binge-watching *Friends* or some other show on Netflix, pair that with beginning a treadmill or stationary bike workout routine.

Add Self-Care rituals. Taking care of your mental, emotional, and physical health is crucial. Self-care rituals like taking a relaxing bath, meditating, or spending time in nature help you recharge and stay connected to yourself.

ॐ

DIY EXERCISE

From the DIY Exercise we practiced in the last chapter, where you set an intention, it's time to revisit that intention, as we will be reliant on it for this chapter.

Pick 5 habits that you must follow if you want your intention to be fulfilled. For example, if you want to start a bakery business, what daily habits would be needed to bring it to fruition?

Off the top of my head, it could be something like:

- Brainstorm ideas that you would need to open this confectionary store
- Decide whether you want to create a physical store or want to order take online orders
- Network and find the right team to make it happen
- Interview and hire the right folks who share a mutual passion with you
- Look for suppliers who can source the ingredients
- Get all the necessary licenses and permits needed to firm this establishment, if needed
- Prepare yourself financially to look after the equipment and the right resources

Your list can go on. After that, think of the associated habits you will need to make this dream a reality. It can be something like scheduling some time off every day to network and find people on online or offline sources. Or maybe look for a bakery chef who has excellent skills in creating eclectic cakes.

By incorporating these small, intentional habits into your daily routine, you'll not only start to see progress toward your goals but also feel more aligned with your highest self. Remember, manifestation is about consistency and alignment.

P.S: The more you practice these habits, the more effortless they'll feel. What starts as a conscious effort will soon flow naturally, becoming a part of who you are.

With each step forward, you're not just inching closer to your dreams—you're co-creating a reality where those dreams are your lived experience. The next chapter will dive into this pivotal process, revealing how to align your actions with universal energy for powerful manifestations.

"You're one step closer."

IX

The Cosmic Dance

Let's imagine you are in a duet with the Universe as your dance partner. This means you're not sitting on the sidelines waiting for your turn, nor are you trying to lead the entire routine. Sometimes, you take the lead, and other times, the Universe guides the way, both moving seamlessly toward a shared goal. That's the beauty of co-creation! It's about partnership, trust, and synergy—working with the Universe, not against it or in isolation. And trust me, once you step onto the dance floor, it's magical.

When we talk about co-creating, we're talking about aligning our energy with the flow of the Universe. We set intentions, get clear on what we want, and then take inspired action while trusting that the Universe will meet us halfway. It's this beautiful dance of giving and receiving—of putting out our desires and allowing the Universe to help manifest them in ways we can't always predict.

And that's where divine timing and synchronicity come in. Sometimes, things happen so perfectly, so unexpectedly, that it feels like everything was meant to unfold that way.

It could be you meet the right person at just the right moment. Or, you come across a book or a sign that gives you the exact message you need. Maybe a song on the radio that perfectly mirrors your current thoughts or emotions. That's synchronicity at work—little winks from the Universe letting you know you're on the right path.

DANCING IN FLOW

Co-creating with the Universe isn't about forcing things to happen on your schedule. It's about trusting the timing of the bigger picture, even if things don't happen exactly when or how you expect them to. So, what are the steps you can take to co-create with the Universe?

Step 1: Emotional Resonance
You've probably heard the phrase *"follow your heart,"* and in manifestation, that's pretty solid advice. If you're not emotionally connected to your desire, it's going to be hard to manifest it.
Why?
Because emotions are energy. And in this game of co-creation, energy is everything.
When I was younger, I remember trying to manifest a new job.
I was fixated on the title and the salary, but deep down, I didn't care about the work itself. I wasn't excited about it. I didn't feel lit up or energized by the idea, and honestly, it felt more like a checklist item than a real desire. And guess what? That job didn't happen. Looking back, I wasn't emotionally connected to the outcome. I was focused on superficial details rather than how I wanted to feel in that role.

The Universe responds to your emotions, not just your thoughts. If you're trying to manifest something that doesn't resonate with you on an emotional level, you're sending out a signal that's weak or conflicted.

Imagine it, and see if it lights a spark inside you. If not, that's your cue to head back to the drawing board and find what truly resonates with your heart.

And, if you find yourself struggling to manifest something, ask yourself:

Am I truly excited about this?

Does this feel right?

Do I really want this?

Step 2: Focus on the What, Not the How
This is where a lot of people get stuck.

We get so caught up in how something is going to happen that we forget the Universe is handling that part for us. Your job is clarity—getting super clear on what you want. The how? That's the Universe's job!

Think of it this way: when you place an order online, do you worry about whether the delivery guy will find your address? No! You trust the process, and you know it will get there.

The same goes for your desires. Focus on what you want and align your energy with that. Visualize it. Feel it. And then release the "how" to the Universe.

For example, when I decided I wanted to move to a new city, I didn't know how I was going to make it happen. The "how" felt overwhelming. Where would I find a place? How would I make new friends? What if it didn't work out?

But instead of getting tangled up in the logistics, I focused on the what—the excitement of a new beginning, the kind of neighborhood I wanted to live in, how I wanted my life to feel there. And lo and behold, opportunities started showing up. One thing led to another, and before I knew it, I was packing my bags.

The Universe works in ways we can't always see. When you let go of controlling the *"how"* and focus on the *"what,"* you leave room for magic to happen. You allow the Universe to surprise you in ways you never could've planned.

Step 3: Take Aligned Action

We've already touched upon taking inspired actions in Chapter 7, but let's dig a little deeper here. Taking the right action is a crucial part of co-creating with the Universe. Manifesting is a two-way street, and action is part of the deal. But it's about taking aligned action, not some random hustle.

It's about moving in the direction of your dreams, even when you don't know the full path ahead. The trick is to start with the one step you do know.

Let me share a story.

There was a time when I had no idea how to write my first book. The idea of being an author in the English language, where I don't even come from a native English-speaking country, felt daunting, and I didn't know the first thing about the publishing process. But I did know one thing: I could start by creating a blog page.

So, that's what I did.

That led to people noticing my work, which eventually opened doors I hadn't even imagined. Then the next. And the next. Before I knew it, I became a published author and this is my second book, already!

The point is that you don't need to have everything figured out from the start. You just need to take the step that's right in front of you. Once you do, the next step will reveal itself. Action creates momentum, and momentum invites miracles.

Step 4: Signs, Synchronicities and Signals
Whether you believe it or not—the Universe is always communicating with us. The Universe speaks in subtle ways—through chance encounters, repeated themes, and those "coincidences" that aren't really coincidences at all.

Once you've taken that first step, stay aware. Be open to signs and synchronicities because they're often the Universe's way of guiding you toward the next right action.

These signs could show up as anything—a conversation with a friend, a quote that resonates, or even a random thought that pops into your head.

I remember once, I was feeling unsure about a big decision I needed to make. That day, I randomly stumbled upon a book, opened it to a page, and the first sentence I read was, *"Trust the process."* It was exactly the reassurance I needed at that moment. Coincidence? Maybe. But I like to think of it as synchronicity—a little nudge from the Universe.

When you stay present and aware, you're more likely to notice these subtle signals. They're like breadcrumbs leading you toward your desired outcome. The more you trust and follow these signs, the clearer your path becomes.

Step 5: Commit to the Process—It's a Journey, Not a Destination
Let's talk about what manifestation is not:
an overnight thing. A one-and-done deal. It requires

commitment. It's a process and every step matters. You need to trust the process, even when things don't seem to be happening as quickly as you'd like.

Manifestation isn't about instant gratification—it's about staying the course, even when the road gets bumpy.

Every step you take, every action you commit to, brings you closer to your manifestation. Keep showing up, aligning your energy, and taking action. The more you commit to the process, the stronger your co-creation with the Universe will become.

&

DIY EXERCISE

This time around, too, you won't need your journal. However, you will still need a piece of paper, a pen, and a small jar or box.

I like to call it a *"Universal Inbox."*

Think of it as your personal system for receiving guidance, ideas, and opportunities from the Universe. I think of it as a direct channel to communicate with the Universe, especially when I am stuck and I really need an answer.

Here's how it works:

Grab a small box, jar, or container to use as your "Universal Inbox." Place it where it is visible to you all the time, where you'll see it every day. Next, write down your requests. Whenever you need guidance or clarity, write down your question, desire, or request on a small piece of paper. Fold it up and place it in the box.

For example, you might write, *"What's my next step toward finding my dream job?"* or *"How can I attract more abundance into my life?"*

And then, release. Once your request is in the inbox, let it go. Trust that the Universe will answer in its own time and in its own way. In the meantime, your job is simply to stay open and aware of the signs, synchronicities, and opportunities that come your way. Be alert and aware, as you don't want to miss out on what the Universe has to say to you.

When you feel you've received your answer, you can remove the note from the inbox and replace it with a new request. This exercise helps you stay connected to the flow of co-creation while giving you a tangible way to let go of control. Plus, it's a fun way to engage with the Universe and invite guidance into your life!

P.S: Check for signals. As you go about your day, look for the Universe's response. It might come through a conversation, a random thought, or an unexpected opportunity. These signals often mirror the emotions you've been radiating, so pay attention to how you're feeling. Emotions are the heart of manifestation—they set the tone for the signals you receive and the opportunities that unfold. The Universe responds most powerfully when your emotional energy is clear and intentional. In the next part of this book, we'll dive deeper into how your emotions can become your greatest tool for creating the reality you desire.

"You are unstoppable."

BRIDGE

X

Feeling It First

Have you ever plastered on a smile, trying to *"fake it till you make it,"* but deep down, felt like a total mess? Like, you're repeating affirmations and thinking positive thoughts, but it's all falling flat? Well, that's a perfect example of how the mind and emotions work together. You see, manifestation isn't about forcing things or playing pretend. If it were as easy as pasting a vision board on your wall and waiting for a miracle, we'd all be living on private islands by now, right? The real magic happens when your thoughts and feelings join forces. It's like a duet dance—you need to harmonize with your partner to make the performance beautiful. Remember how, in the last chapter, we touched on the idea that simply thinking about your desires isn't enough? You can think all day long about the life you want, but if your emotions aren't in alignment, it's like pressing the gas pedal with the parking brake still on. You're not going anywhere!

Let me explain with a personal story.

I used to create vision boards—big, colorful collages of everything I wanted to manifest. I'd cut out pictures of dreamy vacations, fancy houses, and inspirational quotes.

My boards were Pinterest-worthy. And while I loved looking at them, I realized that I wasn't actually feeling anything. I was going through the motions, checking off boxes, but my emotions weren't engaged. I was treating the process like a to-do list, rather than something alive and vibrant. No wonder nothing was happening.

Our emotions are the driving force behind everything we manifest. They're like the fuel in your manifestation engine. Without them, your dreams won't come to you naturally because they're missing the magnetic pull that emotions create.

When you think about what you want, it's your feelings that draw that reality closer to you. It's not enough to want something—you have to *feel* it, too. When your thoughts and emotions are in sync, that's when the Universe takes notice.

Your emotions are the frequency that either attracts or repels what you want. If you're feeling doubt, fear, or frustration about your desire, you're sending out a signal that says, *"I don't really believe this is possible."* And that's the energy you'll attract back.

On the other hand, if you're feeling excited, joyful, and grateful, as if your desire is already yours, you're sending out a much higher frequency that says, *"I'm ready for this!"*

Your thoughts set the intention, but your emotions fuel the journey. They generate the energy that magnetizes your dreams toward you. The stronger the emotional connection you have with what you want, the faster and more naturally it can come into your life.

THE EMOTIONAL BLUEPRINT

I want you to think back to a time when you were deeply excited about something—a vacation, a new job, maybe even falling in love. How did it feel in your body? The butterflies? The anticipation? That feeling is what we're aiming for in manifestation. Your emotions are like a beacon, calling in the experiences you desire.

This reminds me of a time when I wanted to manifest a new car. I didn't just think about it. I allowed myself to feel what it would be like to drive that car—the excitement of walking to my new car, the sense of peace I'd feel as I settled in, and the joy of riding with friends there. I was emotionally engaged with the vision, and within weeks, the perfect car became available.

When you attach strong, positive emotions to your dreams, you're not just thinking about them—you're living them. You start to embody the energy of your desires, and that's when the magic begins.

If you're manifesting from a place of joy, excitement, and fulfillment, you're aligning yourself with the vibration of your dream. It's like turning the dial on a radio until you tune into the right frequency. And once you're on that frequency, the Universe can't help but respond.

Here's where things often get tricky, though. Many people think they can "think" their way into manifestation, but they forget the emotional side.

Imagine trying to manifest a dream home while feeling stressed, fearful, or doubtful about whether it'll actually happen. What kind of signal are you sending out with those emotions? Mixed messages! It's like pressing the gas and brake at the same time—confusing and counterproductive.

Your emotions create momentum. When you're aligned emotionally with what you want, everything flows. Opportunities, ideas, and synchronicities seem to pop up from nowhere. That's because, without emotions, your dreams may just stay in your head as wishes instead of becoming your reality.

PEARLS OF WISDOM

One of my favorite authors, Neville Goddard, truly explained this concept better than most. In his book *"Feeling is the Secret,"* he dives deep into the idea that your emotions are the key to unlocking your desires. He argues that it's not just about what you think but what you feel that determines what shows up in your life. Goddard believed that your subconscious mind, which is the powerhouse behind manifestation, is primarily influenced by feelings.

Your conscious thoughts are important, sure, but it's your emotional state that impresses upon your subconscious and shapes your reality. So, in essence, if you can *feel* it, you can *have* it.

Let's break this down a bit.

If you can imagine yourself living your dream life and actually feel the excitement, joy, and gratitude as if it's already here, your subconscious starts to accept that as your reality. It simply responds to the energy you're creating. It's not about fooling yourself or pretending but about genuinely immersing yourself in the feelings of already having what you want.

For example, if you want to manifest a new home, don't just think about the layout and location. Close your eyes and feel what it would be like to wake up there, walk through the kitchen, or have friends over for dinner. The more vividly and emotionally you can connect with that experience, the more real it becomes in your subconscious, and the faster it can manifest in your life.

Think about the last time you were deeply, emotionally invested in something—whether it was a relationship, a job, or a personal goal. Didn't things start to move and shift in ways you couldn't explain? That's because your emotions were working as the catalyst for change.

MENTAL REHEARSAL

It starts with a practice I like to call *"mental rehearsal,"* but with an emotional twist.

Athletes do this all the time. They mentally rehearse winning the race, scoring the goal, or finishing the marathon. But here's the key—they don't just see it happening; they *feel* it. They feel the adrenaline, the excitement, and the sense of victory. And that's exactly what we need to do in our manifestation practice—feel it.

First, get crystal clear on what you want. It could be a new relationship, a promotion, or even financial abundance. Whatever it is, you need to picture it in vivid detail but don't stop there. You need to take it a step further and ask yourself, *"How will I feel when I have this?"* Will you feel excited, peaceful, confident, or relieved? Tune into those emotions and let them wash over you.

For example, if you're trying to manifest more abundance, don't focus on the lack in your life. Instead, start feeling abundant in small ways—whether it's appreciating the money you already have, treating yourself to something special, or even just walking with confidence like someone who is already financially secure.

I did this when I was trying to manifest more opportunities in my career. Every morning, I would wake up and feel like the person who already had those opportunities. I'd imagine what it would be like to be in demand, to be doing the work I loved, to have people excited to work with me. And soon enough, those opportunities started to show up.

The more emotionally immersed you can be in that experience, the more powerful your manifestation will be.

The secret to manifesting faster isn't necessarily doing more—it's feeling more. It's about letting yourself live in the vibration of what you want now, even before it shows up. This creates a sense of inevitability. You're not just hoping for your dream—you're already living it on an emotional level.

છ

DIY EXERCISE

Here's a fun, thought-provoking exercise that'll help you tap into the power of emotions to manifest with ease. I call it *"Future Memories,"* and it's a creative way to emotionally connect with your desires by imagining them as memories that have already happened.

Take a few moments to imagine one of your dreams or desires as if it's already happened. But instead of visualizing it from a third-person perspective, imagine you're looking back on it like a memory. For example, if you are manifesting a vacation, imagine sitting on your couch months later, reminiscing about that incredible trip you took.

How does it feel to remember it?

What details stand out?

How do you feel thinking about it?

Next, get specific. What did it feel like to wake up in your hotel room, step onto the beach, or explore new places? What smells and sounds do you remember? The key is fully immersing yourself in the experience using all your senses. The more vividly you can imagine this *"memory,"* the more real it will feel. Now, write down your future memory in your journal as if you're recalling it from the past.

For example,

"I can't believe how perfect that vacation was! The beach was exactly how I imagined it, and I felt so relaxed and at peace the whole time."

And then finally, make it a habit to revisit this future memory in your mind regularly. Every time you *"remember"* it, feel the emotions again. Let yourself sink into that feeling of excitement, joy, and fulfillment. The more you emotionally rehearse this future memory, the more your subconscious mind will believe it's already happened—and the faster the Universe will work to bring it to you.

P.S: This exercise is a powerful way to align your emotions with your desires and keep you in a state of expectation and excitement.

Feel the wish fulfilled, and watch the magic unfold. The more vividly you can embody the feelings of already having what you desire, the easier it becomes to draw those desires into your life.

It's not just about imagining—it's about feeling it first and living the emotional truth of your dreams now, as if they're already yours. This is the heart of manifestation.

"You are powerful beyond belief."

XI

Tagging Emotions

Whether it's joy that makes you want to dance in your kitchen, anger that boils up like a volcano, or jealousy that sneaks in when you least expect it—every single one of them is a valid emotion and matters. It's human, it's natural, and a part of the experience we signed up for in life. It's about embracing them, allowing them to surface, and, most importantly, giving yourself permission to feel them without judgment.

I remember a time when I was constantly trying to pose a happy face. No matter what happened—bad day at work, relationship issues, you name it—I'd tell myself, *"Be positive! Just smile!"*

But deep down, I was ignoring the very real frustration and sadness I felt. And guess what? Those feelings only grew stronger because I wasn't dealing with them.

It wasn't until I learned that it's perfectly okay to acknowledge how I truly felt that I finally started to heal. I allowed myself to say, *"Right now, I feel angry,"* instead of *"Right now, I am angry,"* or *"At this moment, I feel disappointed,"* instead of *"At this moment, I am disappointed."*

By naming my feelings, I started to regain my sense of control over them.

You see, every emotion you experience has a purpose.

Emotions like anger or jealousy aren't *"bad"*—they're indicators like flashing lights on your dashboard telling you something needs your attention. If you ignore them, they'll just keep blinking louder. But if you take a minute to say, *"Okay, I'm feeling this way right now,"* and tag that emotion, you allow yourself to process it healthily.

A few years ago, I was working on a project that meant the world to me. I'd poured my heart and soul into it, and when I didn't get the recognition I was hoping for, a deep frustration hit me. You know, the kind that gnaws at you. At first, I tried to brush it off, act like I wasn't upset like it didn't matter—but inside, I was fuming. I wanted to scream, *"Why is this happening to me?"*

I realized, though, that suppressing those feelings only made them louder in my head.

And here's where the magic happened: I let myself *feel* it. I sat with that frustration for a moment and said out loud, *"Right now, I feel really angry."* Just that small act of naming it gave me a sense of control. I tagged the emotion and by doing so, I could move on from it rather than letting it silently dictate my day.

By naming your feelings—whether anger, sadness, confusion or even jealousy—you can gain power. It's like labeling a file in a drawer. Once it's labeled, you know exactly where to find it, and more importantly, you know what to do with it. There's no need to hide from what you're feeling.

Permit yourself to name that feeling, and remind yourself that no feeling is final. This is how we begin to navigate through the ups and downs of our inner world.

So, the next time you feel a wave of anger, jealousy, guilt, or any other emotion that society tells you to hide, I want you to pause. Give yourself a moment of grace, tag the emotion, and say, *"I'm feeling this, and that's okay."* Once you name it, you can start working through it. It's a step toward understanding what triggered that feeling and how you can shift it.

Okay, now that you've tagged your feelings, what's next? How do you actually deal with them? Here's where we dig in a little deeper.

You're not just going to tag and leave them there. No, we're going to work through them together.

Let's dive into an exercise that will help you work through some of the tougher emotions—anger, fear, anxiety, confusion, jealousy, and more.

The goal here is to understand where these feelings are coming from, reframe them, walk through a thought process that will help you gain clarity and power, and ultimately transform them into something positive.

ॐ

DIY EXERCISE

It's DIY o'clock, and it's time to bring out your journal again for this activity. As mentioned earlier, feel free to use the space provided here if you please. I have also worked out this activity myself. So, you will find my example answers, followed by the space for you to add yours.

All you have to do is honestly pen down the answers to the questions asked here. Remember, honesty is the key. If you are not being honest and authentic to yourself, this activity won't work out in your favor.

Give this an honest try. What do you have to lose? Go all in!

Let's start with anger.

Who am I angry with?

(Identify the person or situation causing your anger.)

My answer: *"I'm angry with my boss. He recently gave a major project I was hoping to lead to a newer colleague, someone who has been with the company for less than a year."*

Your answer:

What did they do?

(Pinpoint the specific action that triggered your feelings. Feel free to be as detailed as you can.)

My answer: *"My boss didn't even consider me for the project despite my experience. I've been working at this company for three years, and I thought my track record made me the obvious choice. It felt like all my hard work went unnoticed."*

Your answer:

What thoughts were running through my mind at that time?

My answer: *"Why wasn't I chosen? What did I do wrong? Is my boss undervaluing me? I kept replaying conversations in my head, wondering if I had said or done something that made me seem less capable. This is unfair, and I deserve better."*

Your answer:

Now, in a parallel Universe, reframe and ask yourself: how might I see their side of the story?

(You don't have to agree with them, but just try to see it from a broader perspective.)

My answer: *"Maybe he thought the new colleagues needed a chance to prove themselves or gain experience. Maybe it wasn't about me at all—it was about broadening the team's skill set. I don't have to agree with the decision, but I can acknowledge that it might not have been personal."*

Your answer:

What lesson am I going to take from this?

(Think about how you can grow from this experience. What is it teaching you?)

My answer: *"This situation has taught me to communicate more openly about my aspirations. Instead of assuming my boss knew I wanted this project, I should have expressed my interest more clearly. I'll use this as an opportunity to advocate for myself in the future."*

Your answer:

How do I feel now?

(After reframing the situation, notice how you feel. Has the intensity of your anger shifted?)

My answer: *"After reframing it, I feel a bit lighter. While I'm still disappointed, I can see how this might lead to personal growth and a chance to clarify my career goals."*

Your answer:

What action am I going to take next?

(Decide what you'll do moving forward. Will you communicate with the person? Will you let it go?)

My answer: *"From now on, I'll schedule a one-on-one meeting with my boss to discuss future opportunities and express my desire to take on more leadership roles."*

Your answer:

Let's do fear now.

What is my doubt or fear?

(Get specific. What exactly are you afraid of?)

My answer: *"I'm afraid of starting my own business. I've been in a stable job for years, and the idea of leaving the security of a steady paycheck to venture into something unknown feels incredibly daunting. My fear is centered around financial instability and the potential for failure."*

Your answer:

What am I going to say to my fear?

(Imagine speaking directly to your doubt or fear. Reassure it and yourself).

My answer: *"Thank you for trying to protect me, but I'm ready to step out of my comfort zone. I've done the research and prepared financially, and I know this business aligns with my passion. Fear, you've kept me safe up to this point, but now it's time to move forward."*

Your answer:

What will I do to prepare?

(Fear often comes from feeling unprepared. What can you do to be more ready for what's ahead?)

My answer: *"To ease this fear, I've created a financial cushion—a savings account that can support me for the first few months of the transition. I've also outlined a detailed business plan with milestones to track my progress."*

Your answer:

Why do I trust myself?

(Write down the reasons you believe in yourself. How have you handled tough situations before? Remind yourself of your resilience.)

My answer: *"I trust myself because I've handled uncertainty before. I've navigated career changes, tough financial decisions, and personal challenges with resilience. Each time, I found a way to come out stronger. I know I have the skills, the passion, and the determination to succeed."*

Your answer:

And now, let's do confusion.

What are the options that I'm confused about?

(Brainstorm the different paths you can take, even if they seem small or obvious.)

My answer: *"I'm considering a career change, but I'm not exactly sure what direction to take. Here are a few options:*

- *Stay in my current job but take on additional projects that might align more with my interests (to see if it reignites my passion).*
- *I could pursue further education—sign up for a course or certification in a field I'm curious about.*
- *I might start applying for new jobs in an industry I've always been intrigued by but never had the courage to pursue.*
- *Freelance or consult on the side to explore new opportunities while still maintaining my current job.*
- *Maybe, take a sabbatical or break to reassess my goals, recharge, and think through my next steps."*

Your answer:

How can I explore these options?

(Decide on one or two actions you can take to learn more or move forward.)

My answer: *"I'll talk to people who are already working in the field I'm interested in. I can set up informational interviews to understand what their day-to-day is like and whether it aligns with my interests. Plus, I'll update my resume and start exploring job boards in the new industry, just to see what's out there and what skills I may need to develop."*

Your answer:

What's my next step?

(Choose a small, tangible action to take, no matter how simple.)

My answer: *"I'll start by setting up 2 informational calls with people in the field I'm interested in. This will give me firsthand insight into the industry and help me determine if this path excites me. If it feels like a good fit, I'll move forward by either enrolling in a course or applying for jobs."*

Your answer:

By when?

(Give yourself a deadline. Commit to taking that step by a specific date.)

My answer: *"I'll set a deadline for myself. Within the next 2 weeks, I'll have those informational calls scheduled and completed. By then, I'll also decide whether to sign up for a course, pursue job applications, or stay in my current role and explore side projects."*

Your answer:

P.S: So, all that to say is that life is all about feeling deeply, learning continuously, and moving forward with grace—even when things seem a bit overwhelming. With every tagged emotion, you're growing and letting go of the resistance blocking your way, something we will learn more about in the next chapter. So let's continue, step by step, feeling stronger and more in control with each new discovery.

"You are limitless."

XII

Releasing the Saboteur Within

Let's delve into one of the biggest roadblocks to manifestation, limiting beliefs and resistance. I think of it as a pesky little cousin, who always tags along uninvited—annoying, yes, but they also teach us patience, persistence, and resilience. If you've ever felt like you're hitting an invisible wall while trying to manifest your dreams, that's the handiwork of your limiting beliefs and resistance at play. Or, as I lovingly put it, it's *the saboteur within.*

But how do these limiting beliefs show up?

Those sneaky, deep-seated, ever-present subconscious thoughts telling us why we can't have what we desire or how we don't deserve is how resistance is perceived. They might sound like,

"I'm not good enough for that job."

"I don't deserve that relationship."

"I am unworthy."

"Money is hard to come by for me."

"I can't."

These limiting beliefs keep us stuck in a loop of self-doubt and hold us back from fully embracing our desires. Then there's resistance—this is when you're working against the very thing you're trying to manifest. Resistance often comes from our need to control every detail, from the grand outcome to the smallest step in between. It can take the form of doubt, fear, or an unusual obsession with control.

When we resist, we're essentially telling the Universe, *"I'm not ready for your miracles."* All of these—limiting beliefs, blocks, and resistance—are just ways we protect ourselves from stepping into the unknown. But, there's a silver lining; once we become aware of these patterns, we can break free.

I experienced this firsthand when I was trying to manifest better health. I'd visualize, set goals, and affirm to myself that vibrant well-being was within my reach. But deep down, I doubted whether I truly deserved to feel energized and strong all the time. When a minor flu hit me, my self-doubt surged, derailing my efforts. My limiting beliefs kept blocking my progress, and nothing changed until I addressed those internal barriers and shifted my mindset.

SELF-SABOTAGE 101

Believe it or not, most resistance is self-inflicted. It's easy to get in our own way, especially when we're so fixated on a specific outcome that we start bulldozing through everything to achieve it.

Take this for example:

A friend of mine meticulously planned her days down to the second. She scheduled everything from work to leisure time, assuming that controlling her schedule was the key to success. But all that control left her feeling overwhelmed, anxious, and disconnected from the flow of life. Her rigid approach left no space for the Universe to step in and guide her.

Unbeknownst to us, we end up cooking resistance in our day-to-day life. Sometimes, we want something so badly that we grip onto it too tightly—whether it's a promotion, a collaboration, or a personal goal. We get tunnel vision and push everything (and everyone) aside in pursuit of it. This hyper-focus creates tension and blocks the natural flow of manifestation. Imagine holding sand in your hands: the tighter you squeeze, the faster it slips away.

As a chronic over-planner, I have always found peace in planning every detail. Have you too mapped out every single minute of your day, thinking that by controlling your schedule, you're leaving no room for errors? We have all been there!

While planning is absolutely essential, over-scheduling can lead to burnout and disappointment when things don't pan out the way you wanted. Sometimes, the Universe has a better plan of showing us a different path, and over-planning blocks its ability to surprise you with opportunities you couldn't foresee. It's like telling the Universe, *"I can't trust you."*

Here's a big one—whether it's a friend, partner, or family member, we often think we know what's best for them, don't we? In trying to fix others, we only pull in resistance. We can't manifest what we want for someone else—everyone has their own journey. By accepting them as they are, we release that resistance and allow healthier relationships to flourish organically.

The second we hit a snag, it's tempting to numb ourselves with distractions—social media, alcohol, binge-watching, emotional eating, or even excessive workaholism. These behaviors might temporarily ease the discomfort but ultimately enslave us by keeping us stuck. We resist having a one-on-one with our thoughts. Facing our emotions, though uncomfortable, is the only way forward.

FROM STUCK TO SYNCED

Removing resistance is like clearing debris from your manifestation highway. It doesn't happen overnight, but with consistent effort, you can start to notice when resistance slips in and take steps to release it. Here are some steps to remove resistance from manifestation.

Step 1: Trace the Signs of Resistance
Pay attention to when you feel stressed, overwhelmed, or anxious about your manifestation. These are the resisting signs that you need to tackle. Ask yourself, *"Where am I trying to control the outcome?"*, *"Am I letting the free flow of Universe to work its magic?"*

Step 2: Identify the Reason

Once you've recognized that resistance exists, dig a little deeper. What's behind it? Is it fear of failure? Fear of not being good enough? Maybe it's rooted in a past experience where things didn't go as planned. Identifying the cause helps you bring it into the light.

Step 3: Acknowledge your Feelings

It's important to acknowledge how you feel, whether it's fear, doubt, or frustration. These feelings are valid, but don't let them control your actions. Honor them, then gently release them. Tell yourself, *"It's okay to feel this way, but I'm moving forward, anyway."*

Step 4: Surrender to the Universe

This is the hardest part—letting go of how you think things should turn out. Surrendering doesn't mean giving up on your dreams; it means trusting that the Universe knows the best way to bring them to you. When you release attachment to the outcome, you open yourself up to possibilities you might not have considered.

Step 5: Next Course of Action

While surrendering is crucial, it's also important to take inspired action. Pose a question to yourself, *"What's one small step I can take today to reach my aim?"* Even if it's small, action helps break the cycle of resistance.

Step 6: Reflect on Past Wins

Look back at times when you've successfully manifested something. This is your proof that you are capable of bringing your desires to life. By reminding yourself of past successes, you build confidence in your ability to manifest again.

Let's look at an interesting DIY activity to understand this better.

ಂ

DIY EXERCISE

Here's a simple but powerful exercise to help you embody the feeling of your desires and let go of resistance. I call it "Future-Self Day," and here are the steps for this activity:

Step 1: Set the Scene:
Pick a day (or even just a few hours) where you'll live as though you're already the person who has manifested what you desire. Let's say you're trying to manifest more financial abundance. For this exercise, step into the version of yourself who already has that abundance.

Step 2: Dress the Part
Wear something that makes you feel like your future self. If you're manifesting confidence, wear the outfit that makes you feel unstoppable. If it's financial freedom, treat yourself to a small luxury that aligns with the abundant life you're calling in.

Step 3: Act As If
Throughout the day, make decisions and take action as if you've already manifested your desires. How would you walk, talk, and behave if you were already that person? Maybe you'd speak up more in meetings, or maybe you'd spend money without guilt.

Step 4: Notice the Shift

Pay attention to how you feel throughout the day. When you step into the energy of your future self, you start aligning with that frequency, and your emotions will reflect that shift in perspective.

Step 5: Anchor the Feelings

At the end of the day, take a moment to reflect on how you felt. Write down any insights or emotions that came up. The more you anchor yourself in the feeling of having already manifested your desires, the easier it will be to dissolve resistance and allow those manifestations to come to you.

P.S: Every time you step past your doubts, you're one step closer to your dreams. Trust yourself and the Universe—what you want is already on its way to you. Let's tap into powerful tools and methods that can help you dismantle those barriers, move forward with clarity and break free your full potential. From emotional release techniques to strategies that reframe your mindset, these tools will be your allies on the path ahead.

"Believe it. Achieve it."

BREAK FREE

XIII

Tapping into Emotional Freedom

Emotional Freedom Technique, a holistic practice also known as tapping, is like having a secret tool in your back pocket that helps you manage stress, release emotional baggage, and—most importantly—clear the way for your manifestations to flow into your life.

Whether you're manifesting a new career, a fulfilling relationship, or just a bit more inner peace, EFT helps smooth the road ahead.

Imagine driving down a highway with roadblocks that slow you down at every turn. These roadblocks are limiting beliefs, unresolved emotions, and inner resistance in your mind. EFT is like having a bulldozer that clears those obstacles, allowing your desires to flow freely into your life.

Let me take you back to a few years when I first discovered EFT. No matter what I tried, it felt like my manifestations were stuck in a traffic jam. I couldn't shake this sense of being blocked—like there was some invisible wall standing between me and what I wanted.

Sounds familiar?

That's when I came across a YouTube video that introduced me to EFT.

Skeptical but curious, I gave it a shot.

And let me tell you, it was like unclogging a drain that had been blocked for years. Suddenly, everything started flowing again—my mindset shifted, my energy lifted, and the things I'd been working so hard for started coming to me with ease.

And then I shared this experience with a friend. My friend was trying to manifest her dream relationship. She'd do all the affirmations and visualize the perfect partner, but nothing seemed to happen. After I introduced her to EFT, she realized she had some deep-seated fears about love due to past relationships. Once she started tapping on those fears, the roadblocks cleared, and in no time she met someone wonderful within months.

EFT isn't just about feeling good—it's about breaking down the emotional and mental barriers that block you from your goals.

By tapping on specific points of your body, you're essentially reprogramming your emotional system. It's like hitting a reset button. And when you combine that with your manifestation practice? You're no longer fighting through your old patterns—you're clearing the way for your desires to land right where they belong.

THE WORKS

Let's break down exactly how EFT works so you can use it right away to supercharge your manifestations.

Step 1: Choose an Issue
Start by identifying what's bothering you. Maybe it's fear, doubt, or even something like stress over a work project.

Step 2: Rate Your Feeling
On a scale from 0 to 10, how intense is the emotion? Is it a mild frustration, or does it feel like it's taking over?

Step 3: Create a Statement
Now, create two statements: One that describes your issue, and one that affirms self-acceptance. For example: *"Even though I feel overwhelmed about this project, I deeply and completely accept myself."*

Step 4: Start Tapping
As you say your statements out loud, tap on specific points of your body. These points are like acupuncture points—designed to release stuck energy. Move through the tapping points. Tap 5 to 7 times on each point while focusing on your issue. The points are:

- Eyebrow
- Side of the eye
- Under the eye
- Under the nose
- Chin
- Collarbone

- Under the arm
- Top of the head

Step 5: Stop and Measure

After one round of tapping, stop and reassess your feeling. Has the intensity decreased? Repeat the process until your emotional intensity drops to a manageable level (ideally, around a 0-2 on that same 0-10 scale).

BELIEF REPROGRAMMING

Here's where it gets powerful. EFT not only helps breakfree from the negative emotions tied to your past experiences, but it also clears the emotional clutter that blocks your ability to manifest.

When you tap and use affirmations, you're retraining your brain to let go of limiting beliefs like, *"I'm not worthy of success"* or *"Money does not come to me."* Instead, you're replacing them with empowering thoughts like, *"I deserve abundance"* and *"Success comes easily to me."*

EFT aligns your conscious desires (what you're actively manifesting) with your subconscious mind. This creates a unified, unstoppable force that supports your intentions.

And the best part? It helps reduce any inner resistance that may have been holding you back from fully receiving the manifestations you've been working toward.

The beauty of this sequence is that it clears the path for your desires to manifest more easily. You're not just visualizing your goals; you're clearing the emotional resistance that's been holding you back.

SETUP STATEMENTS

The real magic of EFT lies in the setup statements you use while tapping. These statements acknowledge your current state, while also affirming your desire to change. They're like the bridge between where you are and where you want to be.

Here are a few examples you can use during your tapping practice:

"Even though I doubt my ability to manifest abundance, I deeply and completely accept myself."

"Although I'm afraid of success, I choose to embrace my full potential."

"Despite my past failures, I'm open to receiving all the good things life has to offer."

Remember, it's about acceptance first.

You're not denying the negative emotion—you're acknowledging it and choosing to shift into a new, empowering belief. It's about giving yourself permission to feel what you're feeling while inviting in a more positive perspective.

BEYOND TAPPING

EFT isn't just about manifestation—it can actually have a huge impact on your overall well-being. By regularly incorporating tapping into your routine, you'll start to notice benefits. Whether you're dealing with daily stressors or more intense anxiety, tapping helps calm your nervous system, making you feel more at peace. And, it's a great way to diffuse anger before it takes over. It's like giving your mind a reset button. For some, EFT has been a supportive tool in managing symptoms of depression. By addressing the emotions and beliefs tied to depressive thoughts, you can create a more positive inner dialogue. Healing from Trauma–EFT has been used to help people dealing with post-traumatic stress disorder (PTSD) by releasing the emotional charge around traumatic memories.

At its core, EFT is an invitation to step into a fuller, richer version of yourself, where joy is not something you chase but something you embody. It heals the emotional scars that have been quietly holding you back and helps create alignment within yourself so that your energy flows freely.

When you work with EFT, you're not just focusing on the external *"stuff"* you want to attract. Sure, manifesting abundance, success, or opportunities is part of the process, but EFT invites you to dig into the layers of your inner world first. It's about addressing the unresolved emotions, the limiting beliefs, and the hidden fears that silently sabotage your potential. With each round of tapping, you're clearing away the baggage, lightening your emotional load, and creating space for more authentic experiences to enter your life.

℘

DIY EXERCISE

Here's another exercise to help you feel your emotions and manifest more easily. This exercise is different from the usual journaling or affirmations—it's all about movement.

For each round of EFT, you'll use statements that help you shift from a negative state to a positive one. Tap on each point while affirming your statement. Here's a personal example of mine that I used for attracting success:

Round 1: Express the Fear or Belief

"It feels hard for me to succeed."

"I don't believe I'm capable of achieving my goals."

"It feels like success is always out of reach."

"I've struggled with this fear since I was young."

Round 2: Get Ready for Change

"I'm ready to release this fear."

"I'm open to the possibility that success can come easily."

"I'm starting to believe that things can change."

"I understand that my past doesn't define my future."

Round 3: Embrace the New Belief

"I allow success to come to me effortlessly."

"I welcome this new belief that I am capable."

"I'm ready to step into my power and potential."

Round 4: Anchor the New Belief

"I feel confident about my path to success."

"Success is becoming a natural part of my life."

"I trust my abilities and know I'm worthy of success."

"Success is everywhere, and I'm ready to claim it."

P.S: By tapping into EFT and embracing the power of emotional release, you'll find that manifestation becomes less of a struggle and more of a natural flow. You're not just wishing for change—you're actively clearing the way for it to happen. Let's now unravel another dream-pulling manifestation technique in the next chapter.

"You are stronger than you think."

XIV

Lights, Camera, Manifestation!

Did you ever dream of sitting in the director's chair, shouting "Action!" on the set of a blockbuster film? The thrill of calling the shots, shaping every moment, and seeing your vision come to life on the big screen?

Step into a role just as powerful right now. You can become the director of your own life, shaping the script of your future with the same excitement and creativity as a filmmaker crafting a masterpiece.

Picture this: you're the mastermind behind your story. You're the one scripting the plot twists, choosing the soundtrack, casting the characters who will uplift you, and building toward the most breathtaking happy ending you can imagine. No one else is in control—this is your narrative, and you're both the writer and the star.

Enter the Movie Script Manifestation Method: your personal screenplay for manifesting your dreams.

This method is all about stepping into your creative power and crafting a life that feels as captivating as the movies you love. You start by writing your life as if it's a blockbuster in the making—complete with drama, triumphs, and the perfect resolution.

With every word, you infuse your goals with clarity and intention, letting the Universe know exactly what you're directing it to create. This isn't passive wishing or vague visualizing. This is action—intentional, deliberate, and dynamic, more like a transformative tool for turning your vision into reality.

As you write, something magical happens. You start to embody the energy of the lead character you're creating. You begin to see opportunities that align with your vision, step into choices that support your goals, and build momentum toward your happy ending. The power of scripting lies in its ability to engage your imagination and align it with action, transforming dreams into tangible steps.

Manifestation isn't just wishful thinking or mindless dreaming—it's a deliberate, creative process where your thoughts, emotions, and intentions shape your reality.

Think of it as playing both screenwriter and director. You're not just imagining your ideal future; you're giving it structure, depth, and vibrancy by putting it into words.

When you script your life, you're doing more than just jotting down ideas—something way more profound. You're declaring to the Universe, *"Here's my story, and I'm calling the shots!"* Every word you write carries intention. The magic lies in the details. Every description serves as a blueprint for what you want to achieve.

Picture this: you've just landed your dream job. Can you see the email? What does it say? What do you wear on your first day? Who's cheering you on? How does the office smell? (Coffee? Fresh paint? Success?)

Scripting these moments brings them to life, allowing you to mentally step into your dream before it becomes reality. And here's where the shift happens: your brain starts working to align your actions and emotions with the goal.

Scripting is empowering because it flips the narrative. Instead of life "*happening*" to you, you're in charge. You're writing the dialogue, designing the sets, and directing your big scenes. You're not just the hero—you're the storyteller, weaving together a life of intention and possibility. And the best part? It's fun!

Whether you're envisioning financial freedom, personal breakthroughs, or epic adventures, the Movie Script Manifestation Method transforms your desires into your reality's blueprint.

So, grab a pen and let's get started with the steps. Your script is waiting to be written!

MASTERING THE SCRIPT

Wish to take your script to the next level? To elevate your scripting journey, consider repetition with intention. This means revisiting your script daily. Repetition helps embed your goals into your subconscious.

Example: Before bed, read your script aloud with emotion. To make this stronger, I recommend using active verbs. Avoid passive phrases like "*I wish*" or "*I hope.*" Remember to write with conviction. Example: Instead of "*I want to travel,*" write, "*I am exploring the vibrant streets of Paris.*"

Then, add sensory details. Engage all your senses to make your script more vivid. Example: *"The aroma of freshly brewed coffee fills the air as I sit by the Eiffel Tower, feeling the cool breeze on my face."*

Immerse yourself emotionally. Feel the rush of emotions as if your dream has already come true. Are you excited, like a child unwrapping a long-awaited gift? Do you feel a deep calm, as if all the pieces of your life are finally falling into place? Or perhaps you're energized, buzzing with anticipation and the thrill of knowing your goals are within reach.

Now, hold on to that feeling and magnify it. Let it expand within you, filling every corner of your being. Most importantly, maintain consistency. Keep your mental movie steady and unchanging, as if you're replaying your favorite scene in your mind. Avoid flipping between different scenarios or doubting the details—shifting narratives can dilute the energy you're channeling. Instead, let your vision remain clear, vivid, and unwavering, like a lighthouse guiding you through the fog.

Finally, release attachment to the outcome. Imagine gently loosening your grip, trusting that the Universe is orchestrating events in your favor behind the scenes. Let go of fear, impatience, and doubt, replacing them with trust and faith. And then, anchor your heart in gratitude.

&

DIY EXERCISE

Time to pull up your journal for this activity. I like to call this exercise as, "Ready, Set, Script" and here are the steps:

Step 1: Define Your Desire

What do you really want? Be specific. For example, saying, *"I want to feel successful"* isn't enough. Go deeper, *"I want to wake up every morning, excited to dive into my work as a bestselling author."* Paint the full picture. The more specific you are, the better your script will be. What does success look like? How will you know when you've got it?

Step 2: Visualize Your Story

Close your eyes and immerse yourself in your dream scenario. Where are you? What's happening? Who's with you? Visualization helps you create a rich mental image, which you'll translate into words. Example: Imagine you're giving a keynote speech. What does the stage look like? What's the crowd's reaction?

Step 3: Write in Present Tense

Always script as if your desires are already your reality. This signals to your subconscious that it's achievable and reinforces belief. Instead of *"I want to,"* say, *"I am."* This builds belief in your brain. Example: *"I am confidently delivering my TEDx speech to an audience of 1,000 people who are captivated by my words."*

Step 4: Set the Scene

Bring the world of your script alive with vivid details. Details create a tangible image for your mind to grasp. Imagine: *"I'm sitting in my studio, golden light streaming through the windows, the aroma of fresh coffee filling the air as I sketch designs for my next big project."* The richness of your scene matters—are you feeling the magic?

Step 5: Focus on Emotions
Capture how you feel in your desired reality. Emotions add energy to your intention. Example: *"I feel a surge of pride and joy as I sign my first advertising contract."*

Step 6: Include Key Details
Don't just see the big picture; zoom in. The more specific your script, the clearer your intention becomes. Mention colors, sounds, and even smells. Example: *"My dream office has floor-to-ceiling windows, shelves filled with books, and the faint scent of fresh lavender."*

Step 7: Wrap it up with Gratitude
Always end your script by thanking the Universe. Example: *"I'm deeply grateful for the life I've created and the opportunities that have come my way."* Gratitude magnifies your energy and invites more of what you desire.

MY DREAM WORKSPACE

Here's the script I visualized and crafted to bring my dream workspace to life:

It's a crisp, golden autumn morning. I step into my office, and the moment feels like magic. The walls are painted in serene hues of teal and cream, radiating calm and creativity. Sunlight streams through the wide, arched windows, casting a warm glow over the room.

My desk—an elegant, polished wooden masterpiece—stands proudly in the center, perfectly arranged with my laptop, stationary, and my favorite coffee mug steaming with the aroma of freshly brewed coffee.

I take my seat, feeling an electrifying wave of inspiration and joy. The energy in the room is alive, almost as if it's cheering me on. Ideas pour into my mind like a steady stream, and with excitement bubbling in my chest.

There's an unshakable happiness knowing I'm thriving in a Fortune 100 company that everyone dreams of being a part of. I am living the dream that I had visualized in my head for many, many days.

My heart swells with gratitude for my dream salary and the opportunity to work alongside amazing, friendly colleagues who uplift and inspire me daily. With my work, I am making the world a better place and I couldn't be more proud.

My boss? A true gem—encouraging, supportive, and someone who values my contributions deeply. She appreciates my presence and ensures I am always deeply valued and respected. The warmth and camaraderie I share with my colleagues make me feel seen, heard and celebrated.

Most of all, there's a profound joy in knowing that the work I do every single day is creating a tangible, positive difference in the world. This isn't just a job; it's a calling, and I'm living it fully.

Most importantly, there's an unparalleled joy in knowing that your daily efforts ripple outward, creating real change.

Every intentional thought, every inspired action, every shift in self-concept contributes to something greater than yourself. This isn't just a personal journey; it's a divine purpose that you're embracing with open arms.

This journey has been a testament to the power of belief, persistence, and co-creation with the Universe. I offer my deepest thanks to the Universe for guiding me, supporting me, and showing me that dreams aren't just possible—they're inevitable when you align with their frequency.

Use the space provided here to write your personalized script. You may choose to do this exercise in your journal too.

P.S: If you feel the urge to act this out, go for it! Channel your inner performer and bring this vision to life. Embodying your dreams with vivid detail helps you believe in their achievability, drawing them closer to reality. The more real it feels, the closer you are to living it!

"Your script is your destiny. Write it. Live it. Own it."

XV

The CTFAR Model

Imagine this: you've been handed a secret formula—not a dusty, complicated math equation, but a life-changing tool so simple that it fits neatly into five letters. This is no fluff or pie-in-the-sky concept. It's real, actionable, and wildly effective. That tool is the CTFAR Model, and it's about to blow your mind.

Now, let me take you back to when I stumbled upon this model for the first time. To be honest, I wasn't impressed. *"Another one of those frameworks,"* I thought, rolling my eyes. But, I couldn't have been more wrong! This wasn't just another framework; this was a *revelation*. It's like I found the manual for my brain—something I didn't even know I needed.

The CTFAR Model taught me how my thoughts were driving my feelings, which in turn dictated my actions and created the results I saw in my life. Everything from my career struggles to my personal relationships suddenly made sense. Let me tell you, once you start using this, you'll feel like Neo from *The Matrix*, suddenly aware of the code behind everything.

Instead of feeling trapped in cycles you don't want, you start to see how much power you actually have. You realize that your circumstances aren't as fixed or immovable as they seem. With this model, you can trace any result back to the thought that started it all, giving you the ability to shift your mindset, your emotions, and, ultimately, your reality. It's empowerment on a whole new level.

Imagine tackling a career challenge, not by reacting to the stress, but by identifying the thought fueling it, reframing it, and showing up with renewed confidence. Or navigating a tough conversation in a relationship by first understanding the feeling driving your response. The CTFAR Model isn't just a tool; it's a lens, a way of seeing the world—and yourself—that makes you the ultimate problem-solver.

Once you start using it, there's no turning back. You begin to recognize patterns everywhere and realize that the power to change lies in something as simple, yet profound, as your thoughts. And from there, the possibilities are limitless.

Ready to learn how it works? Buckle up, because we're diving in.

THE 5 BUILDING BLOCKS

Let's decode those five letters: Circumstances, Thoughts, Feelings, Actions, and Results. Think of them as puzzle pieces that make up every single experience in your life. Once you know how to arrange them, you can create any picture you want.

Circumstances (C): The Neutral Truth

Let's start with the simplest piece: Circumstances. These are just the facts—plain, neutral, and uncolored by opinion. A circumstance is something everyone would agree on.

For example:

- *"It's raining."*
- *"I have a job interview tomorrow."*
- *"I weigh 65 kgs."*

These are facts. They aren't good or bad on their own; they just are. The key here is that circumstances themselves don't carry any emotional weight. They're like blank canvases. It's our thoughts about these circumstances that bring them to life.

Most of us don't realize that many of the things we react to emotionally aren't circumstances—they're actually our thoughts about circumstances. The truth is, the weather isn't upsetting. The fact that your interview is tomorrow isn't inherently stressful.

The situation is neutral, and how you think about it is what drives your emotional experience. So, circumstances are where everything begins—but they don't hold the power. *You do!*

A few years ago, I kept spiraling about how my workload was "too much." I'd think, *"I'm drowning in deadlines!"* and feel completely overwhelmed. But when I used the CTFAR model, I realized something huge. The fact was just this: I had a to-do list with 15 tasks. The stress? That was coming from my thought, *"This is impossible."* Changing that one thought to, *"I can tackle this, one step at a time,"* changed everything. Suddenly, the weight lifted.

Thoughts (T): The Story We Tell Ourselves

Now, let's talk about the heavy lifter of the model: Thoughts. Thoughts are simply the sentences that run through your mind—those internal dialogues and stories you tell yourself about the world.

For example, your manager asking you to stay late is a circumstance. But when you think, my manager is so demanding, that's not a fact—it's your opinion. Someone else might think, *'Staying late will help me get ahead'*.

Same situation, different thought.

That means you can choose your thoughts, and by choosing different thoughts, you can change the way you feel, act, and experience life. It's always your thoughts that create your feelings, not the circumstance itself. When you label something as *"good"* or *"bad,"* you're attaching a story to it. This means you have the power to reframe your thoughts and see situations in a whole new light.

Feelings (F): The Compass of Emotions

Here's where the model gets personal because we all have feelings, and most of us spend our lives reacting to them or trying to avoid them. Feelings are those one-word descriptors of our emotional state: anxious, frustrated, proud, angry, or relaxed. Unlike thoughts, which are sentences in our mind, feelings are vibrations in our body. They're not just mental; they're physical too—a flutter in your chest when you're excited, a knot in your stomach when you're anxious. These physical sensations are tied to our emotional reactions.

A common mistake is confusing thoughts and feelings. If someone asks how you felt about your boss asking you to stay late, you might say, *"I'm upset because my boss demands too much of my time."* The truth is, the feeling here is *"upset."* The thought, on the other hand, is, *"My boss demands too much of my time."* Can you see the difference? The thought triggered the feeling, not the circumstance itself.

Many moons ago, I remember feeling extremely anxious about giving a presentation. I kept telling myself that everyone would judge me and I'd embarrass myself. That thought created the anxiety, not the presentation itself. Once I changed my thoughts, I *felt* prepared, and my anxiety turned into confidence.

Same presentation. Completely different feeling.

Actions (A): What You Do (Or Don't Do)

Your feelings fuel your actions—it's that simple. Every action (or inaction) you take stems from how you're feeling in the moment. If you're feeling overwhelmed, you might procrastinate or complain to a coworker instead of tackling your to-do list. If you're feeling confident, you're more likely to take bold steps and follow through on your goals.

Your actions (or lack of action) are driven by the emotions that stem from your thoughts. Let's say you're upset with your boss for asking you to stay late. That upset feeling might lead you to gossip with coworkers, which then impacts your work relationships and maybe even your performance. On the flip side, if you feel determined, you'll roll up your sleeves and get to work.

If you're stuck in inaction, ask yourself what feeling is holding you back. Then trace it back to the thought that's driving it.

Results (R): The Consequence of Your Actions

Finally, we reach the grand finale of the model: Results. The results in your life are a direct reflection of your actions, which stem from your feelings, which stem from your thoughts.

For example, if you're constantly thinking, *"I'm not good enough,"* you'll feel defeated, act half-heartedly, and end up with results that reinforce that belief. But change your thought to, *"I'm capable of figuring this out,"* and suddenly, everything shifts.

That's the beauty of the CTFAR model—it shows you that your thoughts are the root cause of the results you see in your life. If you're not happy with your results, you need to change your thoughts.

When I shifted my thought from *"I'll never finish this project"* to *"I'm capable of handling this workload,"* my actions changed. Instead of procrastinating, I started tackling the work with more energy, and guess what? The project was a success and delivered on time. My thoughts created a feeling of capability, which led to focused action and delivered the result I wanted.

Let's get you to a DIY Exercise to put it to practicality.

৪৩

DIY EXERCISE

Now, how can you start using the CTFAR model in your everyday life?

Here's a fun exercise called the "Thought Download" to help you gain insight into your thoughts and how they're affecting your results.

Thought Download

Take 5 minutes, grab a notebook, and jot down every thought that's running through your head—without judgment, without overthinking. Just let it flow. This is a brain dump where you get everything on paper. Once you've done this, pick one thought that stands out and plug it into the CTFAR model.

Ask yourself: *"Is this thought serving me?"*, *"Is it leading to the results I want?"*

There are two ways to approach the CTFAR model—through the Unintentional Model (which reflects the current state of your mind) and the Intentional Model (which defines the life you want to build).

Unintentional Model:

This model is your default setting. It's what happens when you let your mind run on autopilot. Here is an example that I have penned down. You can take out your journal or use the space given here to do this activity.

C: Circumstance—State of being single, wanting to find someone who loves me truly.

T: Thought—"I'm not pretty enough," "I'm running out of time," "I'm unlovable."

F: Feeling—Unworthy, unattractive, unlucky.

A: Action—Sign up for every dating site, but with a sense of desperation.

R: Result—Continue feeling stuck and frustrated.

Intentional Model:

This model is what happens when you consciously choose new thoughts to create the life you want.

R: Result—A healthy, loving relationship that serves me.

A: Action—Work on self-belief, create boundaries, trust the process, and stay open.

F: Feeling—Complete, confident, loved, and valued.

T: Thought—"I am deserving of love. The right partner will find me when the time is right."

By practicing the Intentional Model, you actively shape your life through thoughts that support the results you want. Over time, this practice helps you align your actions and emotions with the future you're creating. Use the space provided here to work on your CTFAR.

P.S: The CTFAR Model is not just a framework—it's a way of life. It gives you the power to break free from old patterns and create new results by shifting your thoughts, feelings, and actions. So, the next time you feel stuck, ask yourself, *"What am I thinking?"* And from there, the path forward becomes clear. Let's now move on to the last part of the book where we work on *becoming* our manifestation.

"You've got this!"

BECOME

XVI

Elevating Your Energy

Let's be honest for a second—there are times in life when everything feels heavy, right? You wake up with a sense of dread like you're trudging through the mud with no clear path in sight.

It's as if life's challenges pile up, and you're left feeling stuck, unmotivated, and drained. If you've experienced this, you've likely been living in a low-vibration state. When you're in that space, life feels like it's working against you. No matter what you try, you just can't seem to shake the bad vibes.

You are not alone!

But on the flip side, think about those moments when everything feels just right. Maybe it's after a good workout, a meaningful conversation with a friend, or simply enjoying a quiet morning with your coffee.

You feel light, energized, and optimistic. You're able to tackle challenges with confidence, and life seems to flow effortlessly.

That's high-vibration living!

When you're vibrating at a higher frequency, it's as though the Universe is working with you. You're in tune with your higher self—feeling more peaceful, joyful, and capable of handling whatever life throws your way. And here's the magical part: when you're in this high-vibration state, you start attracting more positive experiences, people, and opportunities into your life. It's not just *"good luck"*—it's your energy drawing in what you need to thrive.

THE WAKE-UP CALL

I remember a time when I was completely out of alignment. I was exhausted from work, feeling overwhelmed by everything around me, and stuck in a cycle of negativity. I was drained, drowning in deadlines, and stuck in the *Groundhog Day* loop of negativity. Every day felt like climbing Mount Everest without shoes. No matter how hard I tried to stay motivated, my energy was low, and I couldn't seem to get out of that rut.

But then something clicked. I started focusing on building high-vibration habits—simple things like gratitude journaling and getting out into nature—and everything began to shift. My mindset became clearer, I felt more energized, and slowly but surely, I started attracting opportunities that aligned with my true desires. That's when I realized your vibe really attracts your tribe—and everything else you want in life. That's the power of high-vibration living.

HABITS THAT ENLIGHTEN YOU

When you engage in practices, actions, and behaviors that help raise your energy to a higher frequency, you're not just checking off a wellness to-do list—you're intentionally raising your vibration to a level where you feel more positive, connected, and empowered. The way you manage your energy can literally change your life. Think of it like tuning into your favorite playlist—you know, the one that instantly lifts your mood and makes you want to dance in your kitchen. Like we learnt in Chapter 8, high-energy habits are your personal power anthems for feeling incredible. I think of these habits like a gateway to a more fulfilling, joyful, and abundant life. Whether it's taking a few minutes to breathe deeply or going for a walk in nature, these habits are all about cultivating a sense of well-being, joy, and positivity.

The beauty of these habits is that they help you release negative energy and make space for what truly ignites you. These habits aren't about perfection—they're about finding what fills your cup and makes you glow.

With this, you're consciously choosing to let go of the stress, anxiety, or frustration that might be weighing you down. Instead, you're focusing on what brings you abundance, fulfillment, and peace. Trust me, your future self will thank you.

Alright, now that we've established the importance of high-vibration habits, let's talk about how to weave them into your everyday life. I know what you might be thinking—this sounds great, but how do I actually make it happen? Incorporating these habits doesn't have to be overwhelming. It's all about starting small, building momentum, and finding what works best for you.

Let's start small—because small is powerful. The key here is to avoid trying to do everything all at once. I've made that mistake before, and trust me—it leads to burnout. Pick one or two habits that feel manageable and enjoyable to you.

Maybe it's starting with a 5-minute morning gratitude practice or going for a 10-minute walk each day. Whatever it is, make sure it feels achievable. Once you've built consistency with those habits, you can gradually add more.

For example, when I first started incorporating high-vibration habits, I began with just 5 minutes of deep breathing every morning. That simple habit gave me a sense of calm and clarity. Once I felt confident with that, I added in more practices like journaling and spending time with Mother Nature.

Consistency is the magic ingredient here. You don't have to be perfect, but practicing your chosen habits regularly is what helps you shift your energy in the long term. Aim for daily practice, but if that feels too ambitious, start with a few times a week. The more you practice, the more these habits will become a natural part of your routine.

I noticed that after a few weeks of consistently practicing gratitude and meditation, my entire mindset shifted. I was able to handle stress more easily, and I felt more grounded and positive.

Set reminders. Let's face it—starting a habit is easy; but sticking to it? Not so much. Life gets busy, and suddenly, you've forgotten to meditate for 3 days straight—especially when you're just starting out. And it's okay. This is where reminders and accountability come in handy. Set reminders on your phone, place sticky notes with encouraging phrases around your house, or enlist a friend to check in with you. Having external cues can help keep you on track, especially in those early stages.

I've found that having an accountability buddy—someone who checks in on my progress—makes a huge difference. We both motivate each other to stay consistent, and it turns the process into something fun rather than a chore. After a few weeks of consistent journaling and meditation, I noticed something wild: I felt *lighter*. Stressful moments didn't hit as hard, and I found joy in the little things—like a random compliment from a stranger.

And learn to celebrate progress with kindness. This one is crucial—be kind to yourself throughout this journey. You're not aiming for perfection. There will be days when you miss a practice or fall off track, and that's okay. What matters is that you get back up and keep going. Celebrate the small wins, like the first week you successfully stick to your gratitude practice, or the moment you notice you're feeling more positive overall.

Remember, it's about progress, not perfection. Every step you take towards raising your vibration is something worth celebrating.

Read the signs. Understanding the signs of high and low vibration is key to knowing where you are energetically and what you need to adjust. Your vibration is always fluctuating—some days, you'll feel like you're on top of the world, and other days, not so much. That's normal! But by recognizing the signs, you can take action to raise your vibration when needed.

When you operate from a high-vibrational state, life feels aligned and uplifting. One of the most notable experiences is a deep sense of peace and contentment. You can spot these patterns and pivot. On low-energy days, lean into those high-vibration habits. Breathe, journal, move your body, or get outside for a reset. These small actions shift your energy in big ways. Challenges may arise, but they don't shake your inner calm. You find beauty and abundance in the smallest things.

Creativity and inspiration seem to flow effortlessly when you're in this state. Whether through art, writing or simply solving everyday problems, you feel driven to create. Plus, your self-confidence blossoms as you trust yourself and your abilities. This often pairs with a sense of spiritual connection—faith in a higher power or the bigger picture strengthens your inner resilience.

Conversely, a low vibrational state can feel heavy and draining. Negative emotions like fear, anxiety, anger, or sadness dominate, leaving you overwhelmed. This emotional state is often accompanied by a lack of motivation and inspiration—you may feel stuck and unable to move forward.

Relationships can feel strained during low vibration periods, as you may find it difficult to connect with others, leading to feelings of disconnection or isolation. Stagnation and resistance to change can exacerbate the sense of being in a rut.

Recognizing these signs is the first step toward change. When you notice low-vibration emotions creeping in, engage in high-vibration habits. This intentional shift can help you reclaim your alignment and elevate your energy.

ᛃ

DIY EXERCISE

It's not just your habits that affect your energy—your environment plays a huge role, too. Have you ever noticed how being in a cluttered, messy space makes you feel stressed or overwhelmed? Or how stepping into a clean, organized room immediately puts you at ease? That's because your environment directly impacts your vibration.

Here's what you'll do today. You don't have to pull up your journal for this activity as you are going out today. You are going to go out on a solo date with nature. Natural light and fresh air are two of the easiest ways to elevate the energy in a space. Open your windows, let the sunlight in, and breathe in the fresh air. Spending time outside raises your vibration, so if you can't get outside, bring nature indoors with houseplants or natural elements like wood and stone.

Once you are back, let's set up a clean, clutter-free environment. An organized space allows your mind to feel more at ease and focused. Start with decluttering one area of your home or workspace and notice how the energy shifts. Do you have to attend to a huge pile of laundry that you were supposed to get to 2 weeks ago, or how about that dusty shelf that is screaming to get organized? Even something as simple as clearing off your desk can make a huge difference in your mental clarity.

High-vibration habits are the foundation for creating a life that feels aligned, joyful, and abundant. By incorporating small, consistent practices into your daily routine, you're not only raising your vibration but also attracting the kind of experiences, people, and opportunities that resonate with your highest self.

Remember, it's not about perfection—it's about progress. Each step you take towards raising your vibration brings you closer to the life you've always dreamed of.

P.S: Whether you spend time in nature, practice gratitude, or clear your space, these habits have the power to transform your energy and, in turn, your entire life.

"Your time is now."

XVII

The Secret Sauce

Ever tried to manifest something so badly, but it just seemed like the Universe was dragging its feet? You're putting in all the effort, focusing your energy, yet somehow, what you want is just... stuck?

What no one tells you when you're getting into manifestation: the harder you grip, the more it slips. When we talk about manifesting our desires, there's one concept that is often overlooked but absolutely essential: the Law of Detachment.

Simply put, the Law of Detachment is about letting go of the need to control how and when things will happen. It's the act of releasing that tight grip on your desires and trusting that the Universe is working in your favor. By surrendering control, you open up space for your manifestations to flow toward you naturally. And, that is your secret sauce!

Imagine this: you plant a seed in the ground, water it, and make sure it's getting sunlight. But after that, do you obsessively dig it up every day to see if it's growing?

You trust that, in time, the seed will grow into a plant. This is what surrendering is all about. It's having faith that your manifestation will bloom when the time is right.

I remember a time when I was trying to manifest a collaboration opportunity. I had my heart set on it. I'd visualize every day, say affirmations, and work myself into a frenzy trying to force it to happen. But the harder I tried, the further away it seemed.

I was stressed. Frustrated. Disheartened.

Then, I heard about the Law of Detachment. I learned that by holding on so tightly, I was blocking the natural flow of the Universe.

So, I decided to let go.

And just a few weeks later, the opportunity came to me in a way I couldn't have planned. It was a powerful reminder that surrendering is the key to bringing your desires closer.

THE ART OF LETTING GO

Let's be real—letting go can feel like jumping out of a plane without knowing if the parachute will open. We humans love control. But here's the twist: the more we try to control every tiny detail, the more we block what we're trying to attract. The magic happens when you step back.

This doesn't mean you stop caring—it means you care enough to trust the process.

When I was manifesting a big move to a new city, I was caught up in planning every aspect, from apartment hunting to making new friends. It stressed me out to the point where I started second-guessing the move altogether. The minute I let go of needing every piece to be perfect? Things started falling into place on their own. The Universe moves much more fluidly when you're not standing in its way.

What I've found in my journey is that holding on too tightly to a particular outcome only creates resistance. The more you fight, the more exhausted you get and the further away you feel from where you want to be.

Think about it—how often have you tried to control a situation so much that you end up pushing away the very thing you wanted? Exactly!

We've all been there. That's because the Universe responds to energy. It hears you loud and clear. To let go, trust that what's meant for you won't pass you by. Letting go is like telling the Universe, *"I've done my part; now it's your turn."*

EMBRACING UNCERTAINTY

Uncertainty can be scary. We want a clear roadmap with all the details laid out. But here's the catch: true manifestation requires us to get comfortable with the unknown. It's about believing in the process, even when you can't see the final destination.

When we try to control every outcome, we limit the Universe's potential to surprise us. Manifesting isn't about micromanaging; it's about stepping into a dance with the unknown.

When I was working on a test that I really wanted to clear, I kept worrying about the results—whether I would be successful or not. But the truth is, you can't control how everything unfolds. You just can't! Once I accepted that the Universe had a bigger plan for me than I could imagine, everything aligned more naturally than I could've planned.

Trust the unknown. The beauty of uncertainty is that it allows for infinite possibilities. Your job? Surrender to the divine force and trust that it is working behind the scenes, even if you don't know all the steps yet.

THE DETACHMENT DILEMMA

Detachment from outcomes is one of the most crucial aspects of manifestation, but it's also one of the hardest to master. It's natural to want to see your desires manifest in a specific way, but when you become overly attached to how things should unfold, you restrict what the Universe can deliver.

Think about it like this: if you're clinging to one specific outcome, you're closing yourself off to other possibilities. The Universe might have something even better in store for you, but if you're too focused on one path, you might miss it. Detaching from the outcome means allowing your desires to manifest in the way that's best for your highest good—even if it looks different from what you originally imagined. Maybe what you're manifesting isn't quite right, or maybe there's an even better version waiting in the wings. Who knows?

I once had a colleague who was trying to get a promotion. He was convinced that this particular job was the key to his happiness, and he became fixated on getting it. But when the promotion didn't happen, he was devastated. A few months later, a completely different opportunity presented itself—one that was even better aligned with his skills and passions. If he had gotten the original promotion, he would have missed out on something far greater. This is why detaching from outcomes is so powerful. It allows you to remain open to all possibilities.

PARTNERING WITH THE UNIVERSE

Manifestation isn't just about your personal wish list or the things you think you need to feel fulfilled. It's about stepping into a dance with the greater forces that shape the world. When you manifest, you're not acting alone—you're entering into a powerful partnership with the Universe, a vast and intelligent force that's far bigger than any single one of us.

This partnership requires trust—trust that the Universe hears you, trust that it's working in your favor, and trust that timing is a part of the process. And it's not just about asking; it's about showing up in your life in a way that aligns with what you're calling in. When your actions and beliefs are in harmony with your intentions, you create the space for the Universe to work its magic.

So remember, manifestation is not a solo endeavor. It's about working hand in hand with a force so expansive that it orchestrates the perfect symphony of people, events, and opportunities to make your dreams come to life. When you truly embrace this partnership, life feels less like a struggle and more like a flow. You're no longer pushing against the current; you're moving with it, trusting that the Universe is always leading you exactly where you're meant to be.

Have you ever noticed how things seem to flow effortlessly when you're in sync with the world around you? That's no coincidence. The Universe has its own rhythm, and when you align with it—by letting go and trusting—you allow everything you want to flow into your life naturally.

Here's a little exercise to tap into this connection. Think about something you're trying to manifest. Now, instead of focusing on how it will happen, focus on why you want it. Then, ask yourself: *"Am I allowing the Universe to help me, or am I getting in the way?"* In my case, I imagine handing the reins to the Universe and saying, *"Surprise me!"* Sometimes, just stepping back and inviting that larger force to guide you can open doors you never even knew existed.

౪

DIY EXERCISE

One of the most effective ways to embrace detachment is to create a personal ritual that helps you release control. This isn't just about thinking or affirming—it's about physically letting go.

Step 1: Set the Scene
Find a quiet space where you won't be interrupted. Light a candle or some incense to create a peaceful atmosphere. Take a few deep breaths to center yourself.

Step 2: Write it Down
On a piece of paper, write down the things you're trying to control or the outcomes you're overly attached to. Maybe it's a job, a relationship, or a personal goal. Be specific and honest about what you're struggling to let go of.

Step 3: Release It
Once you've written everything down, hold the paper in your hands and say out loud, *"I release the need to control. I trust the Universe to guide me."* Feel the weight of those words as you let them sink in.

Step 4: Burn or Tear the Paper
Now comes the fun part—symbolically letting go. You can either burn the paper (safely, of course!) or tear it into small pieces. As you do this, visualize yourself releasing the control and surrendering to the flow of the Universe.

Step 5: Close with Gratitude
After you've completed the ritual, take a moment to express gratitude for the process. Thank the Universe for guiding and affirming your trust in unfolding your desires.

P.S: This exercise helps you feel the act of surrendering. It's a physical representation of the mental and emotional process of detachment. By releasing the need to control, you're opening the door for the Universe to bring your manifestations to life in the best way possible. And now, the moment has come to step into the next phase—to truly embody your desires and align with the energy of everything you wish to attract. Turn the page and let's uncover how to become your manifestation and make it your reality.

"Your dream life is waiting—go claim it!"

XVIII

Becoming Your Manifestation

Congratulations! You made it to the last chapter of this book. Yay! Pat yourself on the back. You deserve it!

Have you ever wondered what could be the fastest way to manifest what you want? The short answer is to *become* your manifestation. It might sound a little out there at first, but this isn't just about thinking positively or imagining yourself in a better situation, it's about truly embodying the energy, mindset, and habits of the person who already has what you desire.

If you're manifesting becoming an actor, it means showing up every day as if you're already that successful professional. If you're manifesting love, it's about living as if you're already the loving partner you want to be.

This chapter is about taking that quantum leap from your current reality into the one you desire, and the secret is that you don't wait for your manifestation to arrive—you start living it now. Let's break down what that means and how you can apply it to your own life, starting today.

So, what does it mean to become your manifestation?

Essentially, it's about aligning yourself energetically, mentally, and emotionally with the version of you who already has what you're trying to attract. It's a shift in identity. You stop thinking of your manifestation as something "out there" that you're working toward, and instead, you begin to embody the energy of someone who already has it.

Let me share a story with you.

A few years ago, I was in a place where I really wanted to grow my business. I was hustling, doing all the right things—networking, marketing, creating. But it always felt like I was chasing after something that was just out of reach. I'd get close to a big breakthrough, and then it would slip away. I started to realize that while I was taking all the external actions, internally, I still saw myself as someone who wasn't there yet. My energy was one of lack—I was focused on what I didn't have, and it was keeping me stuck.

One day, after reading about this concept of becoming your manifestation, I decided to try something different. I stopped seeing myself as someone trying to grow a successful business, and I started showing up as if I *already* had that success. I began acting, thinking, and making decisions like the business owner I wanted to be. I asked myself, *"What would the successful version of me do?"* and then I did that.

The shift was almost immediate. Opportunities started flowing to me, clients came out of nowhere, and I was able to take my business to a whole new level. Why? Because I stopped chasing success and started being successful. When you become the thing you want to manifest, the Universe responds to that energy.

IDENTITY SHIFT

At the core of manifesting through becoming is a concept called identity shifting. Your identity is essentially how you see yourself, and it's shaped by your thoughts, beliefs, habits, and emotions. If you think of yourself as someone who is always struggling financially, that identity is going to shape the way you approach money. You might unknowingly make decisions that reinforce that struggle. On the other hand, if you start seeing yourself as someone who is financially abundant, you'll make different choices, you'll radiate a different energy, and you'll attract more abundance.

Imagine you're manifesting a fulfilling relationship. Instead of focusing on the lack of a partner or thinking, *"When I find love, I'll finally be happy,"* shift your identity. Start living as if you're already in that loving relationship. How would you treat yourself? How would you show up in your daily life? You'd probably take better care of yourself, feel more confident, and radiate that love out into the world. That's the energy that's going to attract your partner.

The Universe mirrors back the energy you put out, so if you keep identifying with your current reality—whether it's lack, frustration, or abundance—you're just going to attract more of the same. But when you shift into the identity of your future self, the self who already has what you want, everything starts to change. You become a magnet for the things you desire.

QUANTUM LEAP

This might sound super woo-woo, but it's actually rooted in the idea that there are infinite versions of reality, and you have the power to "jump" from one version of your life to another. Essentially, the life you desire already exists in a parallel reality. Your dream career? Already happening. Your ideal relationship? Already there. And you can access that version of reality by aligning yourself with it energetically and mentally.

Quantum jumping is about collapsing the gap between where you are and where you want to be. You stop seeing your desires as something distant and start embodying the version of yourself who is already living that life. It's like tuning into a different radio station. The frequency of your dream life is already out there—you just need to dial into it.

How do you do this? Start by visualizing the version of yourself who has everything you desire. What does that version of you think about? How do they make decisions? How do they handle challenges?

Now, take one step today that aligns with that version of you. It could be something small, like dressing in a way that makes you feel more confident or making a bold decision in your career. Each time you take a step toward embodying that version of yourself, you're jumping closer to your desired reality.

IT'S ALREADY DONE

One of the most powerful things you can do when manifesting is to live in the energy of *"already done."* This means acting as if your desire has already manifested. It's not about faking it; it's about genuinely believing and feeling that it's already yours.

Think about it: when you know something is on its way, you don't stress about it. You don't doubt it. You're relaxed, confident, and at peace. That's the energy you need to cultivate when manifesting. If you're constantly obsessing over whether or not your manifestation is going to happen, you're creating resistance. But when you act as if it's already done, you're in a state of allowing. You're open, receptive, and aligned with the energy of your desires.

Here's a simple practice you can try: every morning, take a few moments to sit quietly and imagine that everything you want has already happened. Feel the joy, gratitude, and excitement of living in that reality. Then, go about your day carrying that energy with you. Notice how different you feel, how different your interactions are, and how things start to flow more effortlessly.

∞

DIY EXERCISE

The idea of writing a letter from your future self is a transformative way to align your energy with the version of you who has already manifested your desires. By doing this, you're essentially scripting your life as if everything you want has already happened. This exercise isn't about wishful thinking—it's about anchoring your energy into the frequency of having what you want.

Here's how to do it:

Step 1: Set a Future Date
Pick a date in the future, like a year from now or even 5 years ahead. Let's say it's 1 January 2027.

Step 2: Write the Letter as if it's Happening Now
When you write, describe your day, your life, and your feelings in great detail, as if everything you've been manifesting has already happened. You're living it right now.

Step 3: Focus on Emotions and Details
Get specific. Talk about how you feel now that you've manifested your desires. The key here is to let yourself fully step into the emotional experience of having what you want.

My Example of a Future Letter:

1 January 2027

Dear Me,

I'm sitting in my beautiful sunlit kitchen, sipping my favorite green tea, and feeling so much gratitude for how everything in my life has fallen into place. I can hardly believe how quickly the past few years have flown by, and I am so proud of the life I've created.

This morning, I woke up early, like I always do now, and felt so rested in my cozy New York apartment. It's exactly the kind of place I always dreamed of—a spacious, modern loft with large windows that overlook the city. I still pinch myself sometimes when I think about how effortlessly it all came together. I feel such a deep sense of peace living here. New York is everything I imagined and more—bustling, vibrant, and full of endless opportunities.

After waking up, I had breakfast with my loving husband. We've been together for almost 7 years now, and I can honestly say I've never been this happy in a relationship. He loves my scrambled eggs, and we always have breakfast together before starting the day. He's so supportive and thoughtful—this morning, he surprised me with tickets to a show for this weekend, just because he knows how much I love Broadway. It's the little things that make me feel so loved.

After breakfast, we hit the gym together—our favorite morning ritual. It feels amazing to have a partner who values health and wellness just like I do. We push each other to stay active, and it's become such a great way to connect. Afterward, he dropped the kids off at school while I came back home to work on my latest book. Can you believe I'm a full-time author now? Writing has always been my passion, and all my books have been a massive hit.

Every day feels like a dream come true. I'm living in alignment with my purpose, surrounded by love, abundance, and opportunities. And what's even more amazing is that I've created this life by becoming the version of myself who believed it was possible. I've learned to trust the process, let go of control, and simply be the energy I wanted to attract.

This journey hasn't always been easy—it's taken faith, persistence, and an unwavering commitment to growth. But with each step, I've discovered the incredible power of aligning my thoughts, emotions, and actions with the reality I desired. I've embraced challenges as stepping stones and celebrated even the smallest victories, knowing they were proof of the Universe working in my favor.

Now, when I wake up every morning, I'm greeted by a life that feels magical yet grounded. I no longer chase after things—I magnetize them effortlessly because I've become a vibrational match to everything I once dreamed of.

With gratitude and excitement for everything that's yet to come,

Your Future Self.

It's time for you to prepare a script for yourself. Use the space here to write it or do this exercise in your journal.

By immersing yourself in the feeling of already having what you desire, you bypass the energy of lack or wanting. This puts you in a powerful state of alignment, where you vibrate at the frequency of your manifestations, and the Universe responds by bringing them into your reality. When you stop waiting and start embodying the energy of your future self, everything begins to shift. You're no longer stuck in the energy of *"wanting"* or *"lacking"*—you're living in the energy of abundance, love, success, or whatever it is you're manifesting.

P.S: Stop thinking of your dreams as something distant and start becoming the person who already has them. Take that quantum leap. Shift your identity. Watch how quickly the Universe responds to your new energy.

Dream big, act bold, believe always."

Conclusion

Before we wrap, let's get one thing straight: manifestation is not magic. It's not waving a wand, chanting a spell, and waiting for your dreams to appear in a puff of glittery smoke. Nor is it an overnight fix where you scribble something down, wake up the next day, and bam—there's your dream life, wrapped in a shiny bow. It's a process, and like all good things, it requires time, dedication, and a sprinkle of patience. Think of it like baking a cake. You can't rush the oven or skip ingredients and still expect a masterpiece.

And while we're debunking myths, let's address the elephant in the room: manifestation isn't going to work for you unless you're working with it. If you're just going through the motions without putting your heart and soul into it, don't expect miracles. Manifestation is as much about action as it is about intention. You can script your dream job into existence, but if you're not polishing your resume or showing up for interviews, the Universe is going to have a hard time helping you out.

Now, let's rewind for a moment. Take a deep breath and think back to the manifestation you set your heart on when you first opened this book. Maybe it was starting that dream business you've been mulling over for years. Perhaps it was standing on a beach halfway across the world. Or maybe it was something simpler yet profound—waking up every morning with a deep sense of peace and joy, living a happier and more fulfilling life. Whatever it was, bring that vision to the front of your mind. Feel it.

Now, ask yourself: how far along are you? Be honest. Have you taken tangible steps forward, no matter how small they might seem? Have you felt a shift in your energy or noticed the subtle ways the Universe seems to be nudging you toward your goal? If you've truly engaged with the exercises in this book—visualizing, journaling, and embracing the principles of manifestation—then you're closer to that dream than you were when you began. Maybe the progress feels small, almost imperceptible, or maybe you're already seeing some of the puzzle pieces start to fall into place.

And if you're not quite there yet, let me remind you of something important: that dream isn't going anywhere. It's still out there, waiting patiently for you to meet it halfway. Manifestation isn't a race or a checklist to rush through. It's a process, one that unfolds at the perfect pace for your unique journey.

If manifestation had a best friend, it would be gratitude. Gratitude is the secret superpower. It flips the script from *"I wish I had this"* to *"I'm so thankful for what I already have."* And that shift in perspective? It's pure magic. When you focus on what's good in your life, you radiate positive energy. The more grateful you are, the more reasons you'll have to be grateful for.

Let's get real here. Life isn't always a highlight reel. There are days when finding something to be grateful for feels like searching for a needle in a haystack. But even on the roughest days, there's always something—a warm cup of coffee, the hug of a loved one, or simply the fact that you woke up this morning. Gratitude isn't about ignoring challenges; it's about finding the silver lining.

And here's where gratitude journaling comes in. Keeping a gratitude journal is like having a daily conversation with the Universe, saying, *"Hey, I see all the good stuff you've sent my way, and I appreciate it."* It doesn't have to be fancy. A notebook, a pen, and a few minutes of your time are all you need.

Start by writing 3 things you're grateful for every day. Be specific. Instead of *"I'm grateful for my friends,"* try *"I'm grateful for the hilarious text my best friend sent me today that made me laugh out loud."* See the difference? The more detail you add, the more vivid and powerful your gratitude becomes.

Gratitude journaling isn't just a feel-good exercise—it's scientifically proven to boost happiness and reduce stress. It rewires your brain to focus on positivity, making you more resilient and optimistic. And when you're in that high-vibe state, manifestation becomes second nature.

Say you're manifesting financial abundance. By practicing gratitude, you start noticing the small blessings: an unexpected discount at the store or a kind gesture from a coworker. These moments of gratitude reinforce your belief that abundance is already part of your life, which in turn attracts even more.

Gratitude isn't just about what you write in your journal—it's a mindset. It's thanking the barista who made your coffee, smiling at the stranger who held the door, or pausing to appreciate a beautiful sunset. It's a way of life that transforms how you see the world and your place in it.

And when you combine gratitude with surrender and forgiveness? That's when the magic truly happens. You are creating an open space for manifestation to flourish. It's like clearing clutter from a room so that new, beautiful things can come in. You stop chasing your dreams with frantic energy and start aligning with them effortlessly. You realize that everything you need is either already here or on its way.

As you close this book, I want you to take a moment to reflect. Where are you now compared to where you were when you started? What have you learned about yourself, your dreams, and your capacity to create?

P.S: You're the writer of your life, and the script is still being written. Keep scripting, keep believing, and most importantly, keep trusting. Your dreams aren't far away—they're unfolding, one beautiful step at a time.

"The Universe has your back."

"You're destined for greatness."

"Your best self is waiting—become it."